gentle
guidance

gentle
guidance

Marie Gentles

TONIC

LONDON • OXFORD • NEW YORK • NEW DELHI • SYDNEY

BLOOMSBURY TONIC
Bloomsbury Publishing Plc
50 Bedford Square, London, WC1B 3DP, UK
29 Earlsfort Terrace, Dublin 2, Ireland

BLOOMSBURY, BLOOMSBURY TONIC and the Diana logo are
trademarks of Bloomsbury Publishing Plc

First published in Great Britain 2023

A catalogue record for this book is available from the British Library

ISBN: TPB: 978-1-5266-5838-8; ePUB: 978-1-5266-5840-1;
ePDF: 978-1-5266-5836-4

2 4 6 8 10 9 7 5 3 1

Typeset by Ed Pickford

Printed and bound in Great Britain by CPI Group (UK) Ltd, Croydon CR0 4YY

To find out more about our authors and books visit www.bloomsbury.com
and sign up for our newsletters

I would like to dedicate this to my family, but especially to my brother Darren, who helps me every single day. You remind me that we are all in this together, and that light will always shine even in the darkest places.

Contents

Introduction

This book isn't specifically about children. Which might come as a surprise. Really, it's about you.

Children teach us about ourselves just as much as we teach them and without this understanding, behaviour support can feel unsuccessful and insurmountable. 'Behaviour support' means helping young people to understand and manage any behaviours that may be hindering them in life, and highlighting any behaviours that positively propel them forward, enabling them to learn, grow and ultimately be happy. You are an important factor in the lives of the young people that you care for – perhaps more so than you may think. This is a book about how to strengthen your relationship with them (and, as it happens, anyone close to you, whatever their age) and in doing so, establish an emotional connection that helps support them through life's hurdles. And it all starts with you – your wellbeing, your resilience, your fulfilment.

I like to think of a child's behaviour as the fifth vital sign – an insight into their overall wellbeing that offers us a glimpse of how they feel about their place in the world, how they operate day to day, celebrate life's joys and deal with disappointments. Behaviour is their way of communicating what they're feeling and what they need. It affects everything in a child's life, including how they relate to their family, peers and teachers (and how they are treated by those people in turn). For better or worse, how they behave in childhood will affect the adult they become, the relationships they have, the job they get, the life they lead.

As a parent, carer or teacher, it's natural to want to equip them to deal with whatever life throws at them, and this is a guide that supports you to do that. I'll be showing you how you can lay the foundations early on, which will pave the way for healthy behaviours as they age. Or if you already feel like you've reached crisis point, firefighting one explosion after the next, I'll give you the tools to help decode behaviours and reset – don't worry, it's never too late.

Most of us are familiar with the saying that parenting or supporting children doesn't come with a manual, yet there are so many books on behaviour out there. I've often wondered why this cliché pervades – my guess is because young people don't follow a set path, and every single one of them is uniquely and wonderfully different, and this is something to be celebrated. But I believe there is something they all have in common: the right to feel emotionally safe, and with that comes their right to perceive the world as ultimately a safe place, to feel energised and be excited about their contribution to it, all the while knowing that they are important and that they matter.

Understanding behaviour can be a minefield, difficult both to navigate and to make sense of (something I call the behaviour fog). It can be unclear at times whether a child is behaving in a certain way due to a potential underlying diagnosed or undiagnosed medical need, due to their age, or due to them just being children. In this book, you will learn how to support children regardless of whether you think you know the causes of their behaviour or if you are unsure of what the reasons may be. From everyday frustrations to more extreme manifestations, these behaviours may present differently, but they are all rooted in one common thread: a need for emotional safety. When a child feels secure and truly heard, their behaviour is transformed.

Behaviour isn't linear. It's to be expected that young people will naturally test boundaries. They need to learn what they don't want, to know what they do want. The journey is supposed to include bumps in the road: it's how they (and we) learn and grow. Simply reminding ourselves of this can take some of the pressure off when considering interventions. We are allowed some space for trial and error as we support children. It also models to them that it's OK to have some contrast in life, to not get everything 'right', but to be the best that they can be and open to continuous growth. Modelling behaviours to young people is particularly powerful because it shows them practically what you're asking of them, so they can clearly see the behaviour for themselves and not rely solely on abstract interpretation, which can be different for different individuals.

This book is directed purposely towards you. You can't control children, but you can control your response to them, which in turn makes you more influential towards them. My practices focus on activating the potential that every single young person has, so we are not 'doing it for them', but instead igniting their awareness, their inner guidance system, so that they can do it themselves, albeit supported by the adults around them. I encourage the adults around the young people to be consciously aware of themselves, so that they embody what it is that they want for the children in their lives and live by that, thus teaching and inspiring through action and being.

Emotional safety

The concept of emotional safety is far from new and it's not just confined to raising children. We all need to experience emotional safety in our relationships, whether with partners, friends, family or colleagues, in order to feel comfortable enough to be our true selves. When we don't have this safety, we feel less free to honestly express ourselves, to show our flaws and be vulnerable, to admit when we make mistakes and to learn from them. When we can't discuss how we're feeling, those emotions can turn to anger, frustration and sadness – and this is what will manifest in our behaviour (whether you're six or sixty years old). This book is about keeping the lines of communication open so that these feelings have a way of being seen and heard, before they progress into negative behaviours or a fight-or-flight response.

Encouraging emotional safety is one of the central tenets of my approach and it's why my strategies work – because they support children and young people, across the spectrum, *emotionally*. Children (like all of us) want to feel heard; they are hardwired to seek connection and security, but when they don't feel like this need is being met, it creates an underlying anxiety that manifests in their behaviour. For some, this can mean disengagement, defiance, aggression or violence, and for others it can be less 'obvious', such as a need to be compliant in an attempt to please those around them, particularly the adults.

Creating an atmosphere of safety, where children feel able to express all their emotions without fear of judgement, isn't 'overindulgent', neither are you 'making a rod for your own back' or some other tired maxim. When we feel emotionally secure – whatever our age – we are better able to internally regulate and modify our behaviour. I will help you learn to identify the needs of your child and then meet them, so that not only are they happier but, just as importantly, you are happier too. Your day-to-day will be calmer and more connected, and your child will feel rooted in safety, which will allow them to flourish.

For busy parents and carers, and teachers already under strain, this can seem a daunting task, especially if you feel you've reached a deadlock. As a behavioural specialist, teacher and mum, I've been there and I get it, and it's why I have written this gentle-but-proven guide, based on my many years of successful practice. We're not going to get it right all the time (trust me, there is no 'right') but I will show you how to:

- strengthen or reset their **emotional security**
- show that you **understand their perspective**
- **embrace negative emotions** so that the child feels truly heard
- **stay calm** (when you feel anything but)
- model behaviours such as **self-love, kindness** and **resilience** that will be adopted by your children
- **reconnect** after a dispute and move forward
- adopt this type of gentle guidance as a **way of being**
- and learn that by **taking a step back**, things are often not as bad as they seem.

My background

I've always been fascinated by human behaviour, and growing up in east London, within a large, close-knit extended family, I'd keenly observe the behaviour of my siblings and cousins, as well as my friends and the adults around. I'd note the different personalities, roles played and the dynamics between all the different family members.

Years later, when I qualified as a teacher – in my early twenties and a parent myself – my love of studying human behaviour intensified. I started my teaching career in a mainstream school, and I'd often have children deemed 'naughty' by other teachers sent to my classroom. I was curious to find that in my class they completed their work calmly without being disruptive at all. Once again, I began to note consciously what it was specifically that I was doing that meant these children settled in my classroom. It's important to state here that at no point did I 'blame or shame' (a concept I'll be coming back to throughout this book) other teachers or parents, or believe they were doing anything 'wrong'. In fact, it was quite the opposite, I was intrigued by what I observed to be some really positive practices being implemented, but they appeared not to be working consistently. And I wanted to understand why.

After about eight years teaching in the mainstream sector, I came across an advert for a job in a Pupil Referral Unit (PRU) – where children who aren't able to attend a mainstream school are taught. There are many reasons a child might attend a PRU, and one common one is that certain children might need additional emotional or behavioural support, and as a result may have been excluded, or be at risk of exclusion, from their mainstream school. Back then I'd never even heard of a PRU but, given that as a mainstream teacher I'd had some success supporting children with emotional and behavioural needs, I believed I could have something positive to offer these students.

On my first day, I was shocked by some of the extreme behaviours I saw, and for the first time I doubted my abilities, questioning whether my newly found methodologies would work in a PRU. How could I help support these young people, many of whom seemed so dysregulated – struggling to manage their emotions and having upsetting outbursts or other self-damaging behaviours and often experiencing high anxiety. By then I had done plenty of reading around some of the key principles that would later form the foundations of my approach and which we'll look closely at later in this book – behaviour as communication, the impact of trauma and theories behind attachment. My methods also work with children who have special educational needs (SEN), and especially those with social, emotional and mental health (SEMH) needs, as that's my specialism. However, for these children you should always – without exception – seek multi-agency support as well (see also page 253).

When I became deputy head teacher not long after starting at the PRU, I was given the perfect opportunity to trial my methods, along with others already tried and tested. I was appointed the strategic lead on the Nurture Group Project – an intervention developed by educational psychologist Marjorie Boxall for children requiring additional support due to their social, emotional and mental health needs. Nurture Groups focus on language and behaviour as communication, the development of self-esteem and the importance of transition and the classroom being a safe base. In 2010, I set up a Nurture Group model that served an entire London borough – the first of its kind nationally.

It was during this time that I merged my work with the practices of other educational professionals such as Louise Michelle Bombèr, a specialist teacher and therapist, and John Bowlby, the British psychologist, psychiatrist and psychoanalyst who developed the renowned evolutionary theory of attachment (an emotional bond with another person). Later, I also trained in the Solihull Approach, which supports mental health and well-being in parents, children and schools, a model that combines three theoretical concepts: psychoanalytical theory, child development and behaviourism.

I related to all these professionals' concepts, and over the next ten years I honed my practices, and the Nurture Group became extremely successful, supporting hundreds of children with a wide range of differing needs. By helping adults to support the children in securing their emotional safety, the Nurture Groups had a 95–100 per cent success rate year upon year in aiding young people to feel happy and have their needs met.

I then became head of the PRU and had seen such transformational results with the children I'd worked with that I eventually left my position as head teacher to set up a training and consultancy organisation, so I could help train and support even more people: parents, carers, school services, the police and those who work in social care. This book distils the key strategies I've developed over the years so that you can give your child the emotional security they need to thrive.

Using this book

My approach draws on psychology, learnings from evidence-based research and studies, along with my experience at the front line of education. Over the years, I've seen first-hand what works – techniques that help children self-regulate and feel safe. I've worked with children and young adults and because my methods are rooted in universal psychological theories, they can be applied to any age (they will hopefully give adults food for thought too in their own behaviours!).

Each chapter focuses on a key principle of my approach, with the information in every subsequent chapter building on the next. The first part of the book will help you better understand your child and the dynamic within your relationship, from exploring our perception of behaviour, becoming consciously aware of the behaviour *we* are modelling to the children around us, deciphering the emotions behind their behaviour (understanding what they are telling us through their behaviour – even when they're not sure themselves!), to recognising feelings without judgement. You will become an effective and responsive interpreter, which is key to working out which needs to meet in your child. The second part of the book will continue to guide you through practical strategies to build the child's emotional security. I'll be giving examples of what I mean by drawing on stories of the children and their supporting adults I have worked with in the past and providing exercises for you to practise. I'll also be bringing in plenty of examples from my own life as a parent to two teenagers, a former head teacher and from my job training any adults who support children.

I write a bit about the theories behind my techniques because I've found that when working with adults support-ing children, understanding the 'whys' behind a strategy helps implement them more effectively both in the short and long term. This insight allows us to work out what's going on for a child, and I've also found it useful in supporting adults through empathy fatigue (children can drive us up the wall, let's face it, as we do them!). What matters is that you understand the concepts and have the choice to take or leave different bits of advice as you so wish. The theories and methodologies I share are complementary, tending to feed into and cross over with each other, laying the grounding for my big-picture approach. But don't worry, this isn't a weighty tome of a textbook; it's important to me that this be practical, so that from day one you feel empowered to exert a positive influence over the young people in your care.

The chances are, if you have your own children or work with children, you likely don't have a lot of spare time, so each chapter contains easy-to-access information and handy round-ups at the end, which you can easily revisit when your memory needs a jolt. While I'm a big believer in instilling long-term change rather than the instant gratification of a quick fix that doesn't last, there are immediate wins you can start implementing today, which will get the wheels of change in motion. Some examples, techniques and strategies will speak more to parents and some to teachers or adults in other sup-portive roles, so decide as you see fit which you'd like to try (or by all means use them all). I would encourage you to read the book all the way through rather than dip in and out, and that's because you need to be in a good frame of mind to implement the strategies and techniques.

Some of what you read in the book may particularly resonate with you, and make you think of the way you were parented, bringing back memories from your upbringing, or what school was like for you. I speak from experience when I write that these subjects can be very emotive, so at the end of the book, I signpost to additional reading should you want to delve further.

*

There's a lot in the news about 'failing' schools, 'broken' homes and 'bad' parenting, but even without having met your child, I can confidently tell you that nothing needs to be fixed, because nothing is broken. After all, a child is not their behaviour. My hope for you after reading this book is that you will have altered your perceptions, feelings and actions around behaviour, allowing you to view more clearly children's behaviours as a communication of need. This will then allow you to build and maintain secure attachments, reduce anxiety and soothe stress, and you'll be proud to watch the young person in your life flourish via gentle guidance in your support.

A further note

I use the terms 'children' and 'young people' throughout the book, sometimes interchangeably. In educational jargon, 'children' tends to refer to those who are primary school-aged or younger, while 'young people' are teenagers, but this guidance is for all ages. For expediency I often write 'your' child, but this book is aimed at anyone who cares for or has a supportive role in a young person's life, so please note that by saying 'your', I'm not only speaking to parents.

I include many real stories of adults and children I've worked with throughout the book. To protect their anonymity, their names have been changed.

part one

The Mindset Behind the Support

Perceptions, Mindset and the Mirror Effect

Perceptions are the way in which something is regarded, understood or interpreted. They're born out of our belief systems, and our belief systems come from our childhood – where we grew up and who with – along with our past and present experiences. In practice this means that the exact same behaviour or scenario can be perceived differently (even if the differences are only slight) depending on the individual, and the way we act, react or respond will also differ. Tuning in to our individual perceptions is key to successful behavioural support, so in this chapter I'll be asking you to take a step back and observe, without judgement or self-recrimination, how your perceptions have a knock-on effect in the support you give. We'll also look at how adapting our mindset is far more effective long-term than an endless to-do list of strategies. Getting to grips with our perception of certain behaviour is a game changer in reframing our mindset and how we manage our relationships. I promise you will feel calmer and more in control as a result.

Perception: more than one way of seeing a situation

What one person may see as a problem or 'challenging' behaviour, another may not, and that's not only OK, but understanding how and why we perceive things as we do is probably the most essential step in behaviour support. Imagine that you and your partner (or your parents, friend or a colleague) are not quite seeing eye to eye on your child's behaviour. In this kind of scenario what we often do is make a case for why we believe that our viewpoint is the right one. The other person then does the same thing and so time is spent with each person defending their perspective and never really feeling like they've got anywhere in reaching a resolution on the best way to support behaviour.

You may consider yourself or others may consider you to be a strict parent, for example, or maybe it's the direct opposite, and you or others consider you to be too lenient, or maybe it is a balance between the two. Whatever it is that you believe about yourself is correct and whatever it is that others believe about you is also correct. You may be wondering how this can be the case. Well, it's simple, really – each individual will consider their perspective to be the correct one for a variety of reasons. We can argue strongly as to why we believe our perspectives to be accurate, even show evidence to back it up, but there never has been and never will be any perspective that everyone agrees with 100 per cent.

Case study

I had a meeting with a mum, Sarah, and her eleven-year-old daughter Billie. We were discussing Billie's use of technology, as Sarah had concerns about how much time Billie spent on her phone, and she believed that it was making her moody and distant from the rest of the family (this is a really common technology concern for adults caring for children of all ages). From Sarah's perspective, Billie couldn't be without her phone for a minute and was constantly scrolling on social media, which Sarah insisted could not be good for Billie's mental health. When I asked Billie what she thought about her mum's concerns, she responded, 'I understand what Mum is saying, but how can she tell me that I am on my phone all of the time when she's always on hers!'

Sarah was so shocked to hear her daughter describe her as being on the phone all the time and responded by saying that that was not true! She said she was hardly ever on social media and was definitely not glued to the phone the way Billie was. Billie went on to defend her perspective explaining, 'Mum, your phone is always next to you. OK, maybe you're not on social media as much as I am, but sometimes you tell me to leave my phone in my room without ever doing so yourself!'

This meeting with Sarah and Billie really gave me cause to reflect on the power of perception. I too, just like Sarah, wouldn't consider myself to be on my phone constantly, however, when I really thought about it, my phone is constantly by my side and I often find myself mindlessly scrolling. So my teenage children may perceive me as being with my phone constantly, but I don't see myself as being on my phone as much as they are on theirs; however, that's due to me subconsciously comparing my childhood experiences to theirs. Of course I didn't even have a phone at my daughter's age – fourteen – but they've grown up in a generation that is technologically much more advanced. From their perspective it's their normal, from mine it's not, and so I perceive it differently from them.

Challenge your perceptions

It can be a real light-bulb moment when we have the realisation that we can be observing the exact same thing as another person, but perceive it in another way. This is often why witnesses to incidents or crimes all report their findings slightly differently. So if perceptions are the way in which something is regarded, understood or interpreted, the same applies to behaviour. How we regard, understand and interpret behaviour will be different, depending on our beliefs, which inform our perceptions, and the differences aren't just from adult to adult, they're between child and adult too. An eighteen-month-old baby, for example, may perceive the potty as 'the thing' that makes the adults strained, even though they may be smiling! The toddler can *feel* the shift in the adults' responses, such as stress or desperation when 'it's time to use the potty'. This perception then causes them to respond by not wanting to use it, as, from their perspective, it represents stress and angst. From the adults' perspective, they've bought a potty with bells and whistles on, and are smiling and dancing their way into potty time, so wonder why on earth is it not going well?

When my daughter was younger, at the end of each day we would tidy away her toys before she went to get ready for bed.

One evening when she was about six years old, she asked if she could leave her toys out. I told her we must put them away and she could play with them again tomorrow. She was a typically inquisitive six-year-old and so questioned why she couldn't leave the toys out just this once, her reason being that she was building a magical kingdom and didn't want to start all over again tomorrow. I stood my ground, insisting that everything be packed away; I probably even fobbed her off with 'because I said so'. When I really thought about it, though, I realised that it was because I preferred everything to be tidied away in the evenings. From my perspective, I felt more in control and I could relax in the evenings better. It worked for me...

Knowing what I do now, I would have allowed my daughter to keep the toys she was playing with out, but put the others away. This would have met my need for tidiness, rather than pretending that I would be fine with everything everywhere, and her need to keep some toys out, which was perfectly rea-sonable too. I often have to remind myself to take a step back and see differences in opinion from my children's perspective (and yes, I slip up myself, even though my day job is to support adults to challenge their perceptions).

Perception cause and effect

To effectively support a child, it's essential to see them as indi-viduals with their own unique perspective.

Understanding how and why we perceive things as we do is the basis for respecting one another. From that standpoint, we need to be open to potentially shifting our perceptions in the best interests of the young person in our lives, and/or working in unison to reach a place of understanding to ensure they feel seen, heard and safe (and that we do too). By picking up on a child's perception of what's happening, we can tailor our support of them accordingly.

Case study

A teacher invited me into school to help with a young student called Ben whose behaviour had significantly deteriorated. He was 'acting out' and refusing to follow instructions, listen or play nicely with the other children in his class. When I entered the classroom, I noticed that his name tag had fallen off from above his coat peg. I asked the teacher how long ago this had happened and she apologised, saying that it was a couple of weeks previously, and she'd been meaning to put it back up. We then tracked back that Ben's behaviour had begun to deteriorate at exactly around the time that his name tag had fallen off.

From the teacher's perspective, nothing had changed in the past few weeks: she had been in school every day, the classroom was the same and the children in the class hadn't changed, so what had happened to make Ben's behaviour change? For Ben the classroom had been his safe space, he had a good relationship with his teacher and had a small group of friends he played with every day. However, since his name tag had accidentally fallen off, Ben's perception of his safe classroom had changed to, *I don't think Miss wants me here any more. Maybe she stopped liking me, as everyone else's name is still there, and my name is the only one that has disappeared. I don't think the other children like me much either. Maybe something is wrong with me. I don't feel good here any more...* and so Ben began acting out due to his perspective and the reasons he was telling himself as to why his name was longer above his coat peg.

Ben and his teacher were both looking at the exact same classroom, the same children and identical coat peg, but their perceptions were completely different. Ben did not know how to communicate in words that he no longer felt emotionally safe in the classroom, so communicated via his behaviour instead.

Below is an example of how different perspectives, and background context, inform our parenting, teaching or caring.

Case study

Parents Kristen and Gary couldn't agree on weekend bedtimes for their twins. Kristen insisted that the weekends felt stressful because the twins didn't have a consistent bedtime, whereas Gary said that the weekends were stressful because the twins needed more flexibility and freedom. They both strongly argued their case with one another, but could not agree on who was right and who was wrong.

Kristen was an only child and growing up it was just her and her mother in the household. She recalls the weekends feeling very serene and orderly when she was younger. Kristen remembers going to bed at exactly the same time as she did during the week on the weekends and having a very happy childhood. Gary was one of five children growing up. He was a twin himself and had twin sisters, as well as another brother. He recalls there never being a quiet moment at home and it was so much fun! Gary remembers playing with his siblings at bedtime, and as so many of them were sharing a room, they laughed and joked until they fell asleep. He also describes his childhood as a very happy one.

You'll note from this case study there is no right or wrong per se, just different perceptions, each of which are valid in their own right, depending on viewpoint, core beliefs, experiences and circumstances. We always have choices, however, and can change or adapt our perceptions should we choose to. Think now of someone who has an opposing viewpoint to you. It can be a child of any age or another adult. How could their background context or underlying need cause them to perceive and then behave as they do? Even if we don't agree with them, doesn't it instantly feel so much better when we can simply be understanding of differing perceptions, rather than obsessing over who's right or wrong?

Belief systems

When we begin to understand why we and others perceive things as we do, we are in an empowering position to then combine knowledge and experience to grow and learn collectively in the best interests of the children in our care. Tuning into our inner beliefs – where they've come from and how they've been shaped – is a key part of this, because our core beliefs impact on our perceptions.

There are myriad internal and external, conscious and unconscious factors that shape our inner beliefs and how we respond to them, and we get to see some in the case studies in this chapter. For me, and many others, trauma has affected my belief system. From the age of around five through to adulthood, I was severely emotionally abused by someone close to me, who was also a child when the abuse began. Even though internally I had very strong core beliefs, I would often keep them to myself and be extremely agreeable, not wanting to upset anyone. I believed that if I held an opposing perspective, I would be met with strong negative energies from others. I carried this feeling into adulthood, and life reaffirmed my misguided beliefs that those who shouted the loudest, so to speak, would be heard, so I learned how to speak with passion and not aggression, how to talk and to listen, and then balance the two. I gained confidence in expressing my viewpoint, while being open enough to learn from the views of others and understand why they think as they do, even if I did not fully agree. As my career progressed, the similarities between my personal and professional life were uncanny, and I began to really understand that if we can look beyond *how* thoughts and emotions are communicated (for example, by shouting), we can begin to understand that every individual perceives things differently, whether they are a child or an adult, which causes us all to behave differently.

Decoding behaviour

As an adult, once I understood the whys behind my abuser's behaviours, I could see with absolute clarity that it was not my fault, nor had I done anything wrong. They perceived the world to be an emotionally unsafe place and their behaviours originated from a place of self-loathing and fear, which they projected onto me. Once I understood this, I realised that while I couldn't control them, I could control my responses to them. It was very empowering.

When a child is behaving in undesirable ways, it can feel like we are failing or not getting it right, and from that perspective we may try to fix or stop the behaviours in the moment. At a subconscious level, we believe that if we fix or stop the behaviour, then the way the behaviour is making us feel will also stop. Consider this for a moment: how does it make you feel when the young person in your care behaves in undesirable ways? Now imagine if the same young person was to behave in the exact same undesirable way, but this time your perception of their behaviour was entirely different: this time you perceive their behaviour as communication. You now believe that they are trying to tell you, without words, that they are not feeling good for one reason or another. They're not trying to upset you on purpose and you are not doing anything 'wrong'. They are just communicating a need or an emotion, which manifests in their behaviour.

Coming at it with this mindset, you'll immediately feel (and therefore react or respond) differently. Like any habit, adopting this kind of mindset does take practice, and it doesn't mean that you will never again feel any negative emotions when witnessing certain behaviours. However, if you practise this, what you used to feel and what you will now feel will be vastly different, and things will begin to be so much better for you and the child.

Responding from a point of understanding

We have a choice in how we respond to any given situation, and the more we practise, the better we will become at supporting our children. As I've explained, being able to perceive the 'whys' behind behaviour is extremely empowering for both adult and child, as from this perspective everything looks and then feels different, so we, in response, act and react differently. If you're in a situation that makes you feel out of control, like when a child isn't listening to you or following instructions, your response may be to shout in an attempt to regain control, or even to turn a blind eye, as you're too exhausted to intervene. But there is another way.

I believe the core foundations that underpin my approach to gently guide and support are universal to all ages and stages of life, as it begins with a mindset that is open and understanding. In practice, this will lead to an adjustment in how you respond to all sorts of situations, not just those with the children in your life. For example, when my mum received her dementia diagnosis five years ago, so much in my life changed. The way I perceived life and everything and everyone in it changed dramatically, and so my intense journey of self-development began.

Her dementia is very aggressive and so although she was only sixty-five years old when diagnosed, within five years her decline has been so rapid that she can no longer be left alone for more than twenty minutes, and cannot make a cup of tea or get dressed properly by herself. Her mood and behaviour are also very unpredictable. As my mum's main carer, I was propelled into what my brother describes as a 'masterclass of lessons' on behaviour support. I learned very quickly that, due to my mum's degenerative condition, I could not ride on the wave of her emotions. When she was at her worst, in order to maintain the best behaviour support and care for her, I had to be at my best. I had to be the lifeboat in the storm and there are a lot of heavy storms! Instead of perceiving my mum as aggressive and difficult in stormy moments, I perceive her as anxious and vulnerable. That subtle shift in perception was everything. As soon as I perceived my mum as anxious and vulnerable, I was then able to adequately meet her *emotional needs* that presented as aggressive and difficult. Again, this takes practice, and in the next chapter, I give you exercises that can help you manage your mindset and responses.

The mirror effect

The way we perceive behaviour, how we think about it, what we expect from a child, and our beliefs about how they should behave have a direct impact on how we feel. It's no surprise then that, be it consciously or subconsciously, these feelings are reflected in the way we react or respond to their behaviour. This can create a mirror effect in which the young person is reacting or responding to our responses and reactions. We may then be displeased by this behaviour, and so it influences our perceptions, our thoughts, feeling and actions, and creates a mirror effect to which the child responds – and so the cycle begins again.

When my son turned seventeen, we purchased some driving lessons for him. *We* wanted him to begin his driving lessons as *we* thought he would be safer driving than on foot and *we* were sure that he would want that. What seventeen-year-old wouldn't? So, when he wasn't putting in the effort to revise for his theory test, we voiced that he was being lazy and ungrateful. However, it turned out that he did want to do his theory test and his driving lessons, just not in the exact timeframe that we wanted him to do it and his 'lazy and ungrateful' behaviour was telling us without words, *What about what I want? I'm not lazy, nor ungrateful, and I don't know how to tell you because I'm not sure why, but I just don't feel motivated to do it right now.* Once again, looking back, I can now see that we would have felt more in control if he had operated within our timeframe, as I could have mentally relaxed more, knowing that he could drive and was safe. Once again, from my perspective, as with my daughter tidying her room in the evening, it worked for me.

We expected our son to demonstrate gratitude to us by acting joyful and eager. For me this expectation stemmed from me remembering when I was seventeen, when my parents similarly bought driving lessons for me. I most prob-ably wanted to recreate an almost identical scenario with my child, as I recall feeling really happy and eager, and I wanted this good feeling for my son too (nothing wrong in that). But my beliefs regarding how he *should* have behaved, when he did not behave as expected, impacted directly on how I felt not only about the behaviour but about my son. *I cannot believe, after all we've done for him, he could act so ungratefully. Does this mean that this is part of his personality? Have we done something wrong?* And so the thoughts spiral, and feelings of failure, then concern, frustration and annoyance emerge, and before I knew it, I was reacting from a place of negative emotion. This reaction was communicated in voicing thoughts of laziness and ungratefulness, and of course my son picked up on what he would perceive to be an 'attack' on him and 'attacked' back. His response then confirmed to me my origi-nal accusations and thoughts about him and his behaviour, and so the thought–feeling–action cycle (which we'll focus on in the next chapter) begins again. No one 'wins', no one feels good, but most importantly, no one identifies the real reasons beneath the surface behaviour, which is the only route to proper resolution.

It can be hard to accept someone's perception when it feels far removed from our own. I often say, 'It's not the truth that you are seeing, it's your perception of what the truth is.' This concept is vital as an initial step in behaviour support (whatever the age of the child) to avoid telling a child (or anyone, really) that their version of 'the truth' is wrong because it disagrees with our own. It's not about letting the child 'rule the roost' but about allowing them to learn safely without unintentionally disregarding their perceptions, instead giving them the freedom to ignite their own inner guidance system.

When someone wants something in life, it is for the *feeling* they think they will get once they have it – we all seek emotional connection in one way or another. You've heard the stories of people winning the lottery, for example. Prior to their win they perceived that they'd feel on top of the world in the event of winning, that nothing in life could possibly be better, but they're shocked that, despite their newfound wealth, many of them end up feeling far more miserable than they did before their win. This is because some people hold the belief that the money will make them happy; however, it is the feeling they believe the lottery will generate that they're really seeking. A feeling of freedom, a feeling of choice or options, a feeling of liberation, and so on. So, if someone wins the lottery but no longer knows who they can trust, they may feel trapped instead of free, or feel limited instead of having options, or repressed instead of liberated. It is the *feeling* we are all seeking in everything we do.

TRY IT: *spend an hour making a list of anything that you want, and write down the feeling behind the reason for wanting it. It could be a coffee in the morning, a reply from a text message, a seat on the train, and so on.*

Now think of a two-year-old throwing a tantrum when their toy has been taken, or a twelve-year-old being rude when their phone has been confiscated, and consider the 'whys' beyond the tantrum or the rudeness. What *feeling* did they have when they had their toy or phone and what *feeling* do they have once it has been removed? Next, consider from the list you created of things that you want, how you would feel if you were told you couldn't have your coffee for a week, or when you're desperate for that train seat on the way home and you realise you will have to stand for the next forty minutes? How annoying!

We react emotionally to things all the time; however, generally, as we get older we learn to communicate our emotions in more desirable ways, despite the way we feel inside. So how you feel if you're told you cannot have your coffee may be similar to how a toddler feels when they are told they cannot have their toy – even the intensity of the feeling may be the same – but it is unlikely that you would throw yourself on the floor and cry. The way the behaviour manifests and is communicated varies with each individual and young people are more likely to communicate their feelings differently. Take a closer look at these examples from this new perspective:

The two-year-old perspective: *My toy makes me feel happy and content, but now I feel frustrated and annoyed. Communication of feeling = tantrum behaviour: crying or throwing themselves on the floor.*

Your perspective: *That coffee helps me to feel happy and content, but now I feel frustrated and annoyed. Communication of feeling = tantrum behaviour: snapping at colleagues/family members or being short-tempered.*

When the feeling we are seeking is not fulfilled, our behaviour can be affected; it just looks different for each individual, young or old. Be really truthful with yourself for a moment and think about when you last had a 'tantrum'. It may not look the same as a two-year-old's tantrum, but we've all experienced the *feeling* of frustration and annoyance, which then impacts on how we've acted or reacted – it's absolutely normal. We need to support children to understand that there is nothing wrong with them for feeling what they feel. We want to encourage them to identify their feelings and why they may feel as they do. Our roles are then to support them to not behave in undesirable ways when they feel certain feelings – if they feel guilt or shame for having disappointed you due to their undesirable behaviour, those feelings can inadvertently lead to more undesirable behaviours.

It's clear our personal perspectives impact how we think about something and how we act, react or respond. As we've seen, no two perspectives will be identical, so how one person feels about something from their perceptive may be slightly or entirely different from how another person feels from their per-spective, whether that is another adult, or the child or young person in your care. The aim is never to get one to agree with the other, but just to understand that how we regard, understand or interpret things will be different, and from there work together in the best interests of the young person.

Supporting from a different perspective

Let's imagine the emotions of a child on a scale. If we all want and need to essentially feel good, the **emotional connection** is what will balance the scale to achieve **emotional balance.** Imagine one side of a scale, heavily weighted with a lot of heavy emotions such as anger, sadness, anxiety or fear. These feelings then manifest as undesirable behaviours, as they are all expressions of emotion.

To balance the other side of the scale, the child or young person needs a lot of emotional connection. Any undesirable behaviours, whether low, medium or high on one end of the scale, originate from negative emotions. This means there's an *equal* level of *need* for effectively the opposite of such emotions on the other end of the scale, such as happiness, hope and enthusiasm, to counterbalance and, ultimately, help the young person feel differently in order to behave differently.

Seeing it in this way allows us to alter our perception of the child's behaviour and then how we respond to it; how we respond reduces the risk of the behaviour reoccurring and escalating in the same way.

Case study

Three-year-old Mya's behaviour went through the roof when her baby brother was born. Her parents perceived the addition to the family as a beautiful bundle of joy, but Mya perceived her baby brother as an attention stealer! He stole all the attention away from her, and not just with Mummy and Daddy, but with her favourite uncle, Jim, her next-door neighbour – even the lady in the corner shop ignored her and went straight to him first. It made Mya feel frightened and anxious that everything had changed for ever, even though Amy, her mum, told her that she was still their special little girl. As Mya's feelings grew, so did her behaviour. She communicated her anxiety by crying loudly for extended periods of time, throwing her toys across the room and on occasion pulling her baby brother's hair. On Mya's emotional scale, the side laden with fear and anxiety was getting heavier as weeks and months passed and her baby brother grew. When Amy would tell Mya that she was still their special little girl, it added some weight to the opposite end of the scale, but not enough to fully counterbalance, as Mya's confused emotions around her brother were so heavy at that time.

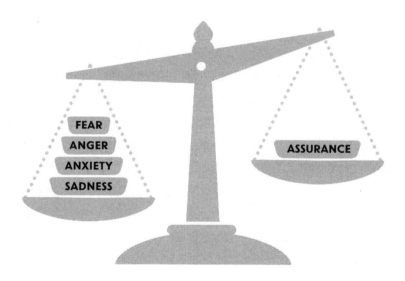

Mya needed to consistently feel seen, heard and safe in order to feel differently and so behave differently. With support, Amy was able to understand how and why Mya regarded, understood and interpreted her brother's existence as she did, which was very different to how Amy anticipated it would be when she was pregnant, believing that she had done all she could to prepare Mya. From Amy's perspective she had ensured that her daughter felt seen, heard, safe and included during the pregnancy and after the birth, and indeed she had done so. Both mother's and daughter's perspectives were correct in their own right. However, Amy came to understand that Mya's three-year-old perception of her brother was as an attention stealer, and these feelings then impacted on how she acted, reacted and responded to her beautiful baby brother. Amy could not force Mya to see her brother the way they did, nor force her not to feel as she did. The only way she could understand Mya's feelings, and therefore her undesirable behaviour, was to counterbalance her feelings. Later in the book we'll be looking at more ways to do this.

Remember, our aim is not to get one to agree with the other, but just to understand that how we regard, understand or interpret things will always be different. If we can practise this, children will feel better understood, and when they feel seen, heard and safe, that automatically provides the emotional connection that tips the scales.

As you can see from the scales, the negative emotions haven't disappeared – they're just now counterbalanced or outweighed with more positive emotions. Our focus is on providing more of what we want to see – more kindness, sharing, thoughtfulness, effort, consideration and so on – rather than behaviours we don't. One of the reasons behaviour support feels so difficult at times is because we are trying to stop or eliminate behaviours because they do not feel good for the child or for us and, of course, we just want the best for the child. However, it is not realistic to stamp out all negative feelings – they are a natural part of life. If we can help children to perceive them as such and not be 'scared' of how negative emotions feel, in time they can learn how to navigate life using their own inner guidance system, rather than just doing as they're told.

We want children to tune in to their instinct from as young an age as possible, so we often say to young children, 'If a stranger approaches you, it doesn't feel right, so if they tell you to go with them, don't go,' or to older children we may say, 'If you feel uncomfortable when your friends are pressuring you to do something, then trust the feeling that it doesn't feel right and don't do it.' In order for them to master managing their own feelings, we need to then understand that the undesirable behaviours are a manifestation of negative feelings, and so support them to learn and grow from this perspective. We need to give our children the tools to listen to their gut instincts, because this will protect them in different scenarios throughout their lives.

From this moment on, we can be mindful that children and young people's undesirable behaviours are alerting us to their need for emotional support and connection. By adopting this mindset, we can help to offer a counterbalance, tipping the scales, while assisting them to learn and grow. It is so very empowering when this becomes almost second nature and you see the growth in your children, but I must emphasise that it takes continual practice. Even now I continue to practise this mindset on a daily basis in order to not only do the work that I do, but to raise my two children in the most stress-free way possible for all of us (and it works!).

No blame, no shame

I'll be repeating this mantra so often throughout the book, just you wait!

Guilt can play a huge factor when supporting young people with their behaviour, as we question ourselves as to whether we have done something 'wrong' or if we're not getting it 'right'. I feel very strongly that we should not blame or shame ourselves or others for what we believe we should or should not have done in the past, or what we believe we should or should not be doing now. Keep this mantra in mind while we consider our perceptions and beliefs that we may project onto the young people in our lives, and how that impacts them and influences their behaviour.

As you know, I have two teenage children and I also care for my mum, who has dementia. I still have moments when I feel guilty about how caring for my mum full time sometimes makes me feel so emotionally drained and overwhelmed. Similarly, in raising two teenagers, sometimes I feel gripped by feelings of worry and angst, leading me to crave a moment of mental rest. Nearly all emotions that manifest as behaviours that I support others with, I've had personal experience of: grief, overwhelm, anger, frustration, shame, anxiety and fear (and the list goes on). It's my own experience that has made me so passionate about sharing knowledge that empowers and uplifts when managing and supporting such feelings and, in turn, behaviours. I feel deeply that we all have the right to feel emotionally safe, and guilt and shame stunt those feelings.

Remember, it is OK to:

- feel negative emotions sometimes,
- make a mistake,
- feel like you're not getting it right,
- regret doing something.

It is safe to:

- try again,
- not know it all,
- change your mind, should you choose to.

And it is safe for children and young people to understand this.

So remember, no blame, no shame, as we explore this.

Mirroring in our responses

Changing how we respond to the emotions behind the behaviours in the young people in our care places us in a position to consistently, positively influence and support them.

Children learn more from what they see than from what they hear. Most experts agree that a very large percentage of all communication is nonverbal and current scientific estimates are that 95 per cent of brain activity is unconscious,[*] so there are so many nuances that can create a mirror effect that we may not even be consciously aware of. From a child's perspective, they are picking up on it and may find it difficult to modify behaviour, or accept support from us if something about what they are seeing or hearing contradicts what they are being told. It can be very confusing, for example, when a parent or teacher shouts, 'How dare you raise your voice to me!' In that moment the young person may only hear that the instruction is being given in a raised voice.

---

[*] Emma Young, 'Lifting the lid on the unconscious', *New Scientist*, 25 July 2018, www.newscientist.com/article/mg23931880-400-lifting-the-lid-on-the-unconscious/

Let's look at some scenarios from a mirror-effect perspective:

'I just want my toddler to not cry constantly,' a mother told me as she bounced her two-year-old son on her knee and he screamed, her eyes red from crying due to concern for her beautiful boy.

'She's so nervous and anxious – we're worried about how she will cope in secondary school,' the father of an eleven-year-old bravely confessed as he nervously bounced his leg up and down (something I was told he did when highly stressed or anxious and that it seemed to have got worse recently).

'He's so unpredictable.' The mother of a five-year-old explained that they constantly had to adapt to their son's demands, depending on his changeable mood throughout the day, in order to avoid an outburst.

'She is so moody and angry all the time!' said the teacher (whose face was flushed with annoyance and frustration) of a fourteen-year-old girl.

'I want nothing more than for him to be happy,' the sad and worried parents of a seventeen-year-old boy confided in me.

If any of these examples resonate with you, remember no blame, no shame – we're just bringing it into our conscious awareness so that we can do something different, should we choose to. Commonly, our first reaction upon reading these examples may be to think, *No, not me, I don't do any of those things,* or, *But of course I became annoyed and frustrated after my teenage student was moody and angry.*

Do note here that you are not the reason a child is behaving as they are, but as a significant adult in their life they will be seeking emotional connection and learning emotional balance from you. One of the biggest ways that children learn is via observation and then imitation. Since scientists discovered mirror neurons located in the brain, it has been said that our understanding of an action and then being able to mirror the same action is really important when thinking about learning and emotional intelligence.

With this in mind, we must ourselves have the things we want for the young people in our care. We can achieve general emotional balance if we feel emotionally seen, heard and safe. If we feel all of these things, we can then more easily and readily feel some of the most common positive emotions, such as joy, love, hope and gratitude – emotions that counterbalance or tip the scales. Let's look closer at one of my client examples from earlier:

Case study

'He's so unpredictable.' The mother of a five-year-old explained that they constantly had to adapt to their son's demands, depending on his changeable mood throughout the day, in order to avoid an outburst.

Tanya came to see me after years of trying to figure out if there was something that she should be concerned about when it came to her son Taylor. She described him as hyperactive, constantly on the go, and always keen to get his own way. While many people had told her his high energy was a phase he'd grow out of, others, including her mother, had said that he'd need to calm down and modify his behaviour before starting school. Tanya also tearfully told me that he is a wonderful boy and can be really loving and kind (of which I had no doubt).

The first thing Tanya and I explored together were perceptions. She became aware of how heavy the opinion of others was weighing on her, especially her mother's. She concluded that those opinions were just adding to her confusion and making her feel like she was failing in some way. We respectfully put the opinions of others to one side, because as we looked at earlier in this chapter, the way we all regard, understand and interpret behaviour is different. She was able to tell me that she just wanted Taylor to be happy and settled. I asked Tanya if Taylor was able to articulate from his perspective if he felt that his mother was happy, what would he say? Tanya said at the moment he'd probably say not very often. She quickly went on to tell me that was only because of how stressed she'd been feeling, and once Taylor was more settled, she would feel far more relaxed and happy.

We are never as effective in unhappiness as we are in joy. So Tanya claiming that she would feel happy when she knew her son was happy is like driving with the handbrake on — she's still moving, and she'll eventually reach her destination, but it will take far, far longer and be an uncomfortable journey. With the handbrake off before you drive, you'll have a much smoother and quicker trip overall. I reminded Tanya that one of the biggest ways that children learn is via observation and then imitation, so if she was unhappy, it would be more difficult to support her son to be happy. She might get there eventually, but it would take far longer and likely feel a bit like an uphill struggle. Whereas if she modelled the happiness she so desperately wanted for him, it would be a much smoother journey.

Taylor was seeking emotional connection and balance in his own way. Like all children, he wanted to feel seen, heard and safe. He was achieving the feelings of being seen and heard via his unpredictable behaviour. Taylor knew for sure that every time he acted in an undesirable way, his mum would become very stressed and frustrated with him. Now while that wasn't the best feeling for either of them, knowing he would be seen and heard was guaranteed and so that emotional need was met, although only in the short term. This would lead to Taylor feeling safe in the certainty that this would happen. This is so very common with children — they get their needs met faster, as Taylor did, because they are momentarily seen and heard, and feel safe in their undesirable behaviour patterns. Taylor was desperately trying to emotionally balance on the scale himself, albeit fleetingly and undesirably, and the reason why the behaviours continued and escalated over the years is because although those particular behaviours may be undesirable, at least the situation was predictable (and predictability can feel safer than the unknown). When Tanya understood this, she was able to support Taylor to emotionally balance and this then became predictable for him, providing a feeling of security and safety. In time, Taylor no longer needed to meet his needs in undesirable ways, and his behaviour significantly improved.

Young people will seek to meet their needs of emotional connection in their own way, usually the only ways they know how, even if certain behaviours they exhibit are undesirable. If they are in a pattern or cycle of behaviour, it is the knowing and predictability that gets their needs met faster, albeit for short bursts at a time. The feeling is similar to an adrenalin rush – it can feel high and exciting at the time, until the crash comes, which feels so much worse than before. They then try to reach an even higher feeling, which can't be sustained, so the highs may become higher, but the lows will be lower.

If any of what you've read here is resonating with you or making you question your previous reactions or responses to your children, remember: no blame, no shame. Just having this awareness of the mirror effect, combined with the understanding that when we perceive differently, we behave differently, is a huge initial step in behaviour support.

Perception reflection

We need to shift our focus so that it's not about changing the *behaviour* of children but instead changing how we respond to the *emotions* that manifest as behaviours. In doing this, we not only master our own feelings and emotional balance, but also consistently, positively influence and support the behaviour of our children over time, by modelling what emotional balance looks like to them.

It can be very confusing for children to know what the 'right' thing is. Should they comply with those who shout the loudest, those who are the sternest, the strictest, or the most fun? And what if their parents say or believe something different from what their teachers say, or vice versa, what then?

How do you decide who to please? Ultimately, in that way, someone will always be left disappointed. Instead, we could support children to understand their feelings and become more emotionally balanced, so that they tune in to their own perspectives and communicate them in more desirable ways. To be who they want to be as an individual while still being part of a collective – a family unit, a school community, and part of society as a whole.

A teacher or parent is only as effective as their understanding of where the young person is. If we teach solely from our perspective, then we may feel that we are constantly trying but never actually getting anywhere. How we perceive children's behaviour will ultimately impact on how we support them. A parent who initially perceives their child as demanding or controlling could alter their perception of the behaviour to understand that the child is seeking a *feeling* of control because they feel out of control.

Case study

I started working alongside a teacher, Roy, with a situation with his student, Matt, that he was finding challenging to navigate. Matt would constantly call out or talk over Roy in the classroom and roll his eyes or look away when Roy addressed him. As a result, Roy perceived Matt as arrogant and rude.

In helping Roy resolve this stressful dynamic, I was keen for him to become consciously aware of his perceptions and to see behaviour as a form of communication – in this scenario, it was clear Matt was seeking attention. We discussed how Matt may have been seeking a feeling of recognition because he'd been feeling unseen and unheard. For Matt, being recognised or noticed fed into him feeling valued, and feeling unseen was knocking his confidence and self-worth.

Roy, after receiving some guidance on what I call the Five Cs (listed on page 46) — communication, calm, curious, connect and convey — began to change his perception and so too his thoughts about Matt's behaviour. He understood that Matt's behaviour was communicating a need for emotional connection. With this in mind, when Matt entered his classroom, Roy remained calm because he perceived it as an opportunity to support learning and growth. This is the mindset needed for effective behaviour support. Roy became curious instead of furious with Matt, and pondered what feeling Matt might be seeking. Roy practised this over and over as he reminded himself that negative emotions can manifest as negative behaviours.

To help with this, I asked Roy to think about what feelings Matt's current behaviour was trying to achieve. Then I suggested he think of the opposite of those feelings — as that was likely what Matt was lacking and therefore seeking. So, in this case, Matt's arrogance and rudeness by playing the class clown could mean that he is trying to achieve a feeling of recognition and worthiness via behaviours that fleetingly get him recognised and make him feel worthy.

Next, Roy thought about how to connect and counterbalance Matt's emotions by meeting his need to be seen and heard. He decided to recognise Matt before Matt felt the need to ensure that everyone in the class recognised him. He spoke to Matt out of class time, telling him he'd noticed he was very knowledgeable on a particular topic and asked him if he'd like to take the lead in sharing his knowledge with the rest of the class. Finally, Roy continuously conveyed via modelling that he was happy to have Matt in his class. Even when Matt pushed the boundaries or slipped back into old behaviour patterns, Roy expressed emotional balance by maintaining his happiness to see Matt (regardless of his behaviour). He continued to speak with him one to one outside of the lesson at other points in the school day to build on their professional emotional connection.

Over time, as Roy ensured that Matt's need to feel recognised and worthy was met, Matt modified his behaviour. At times Roy described it as two steps forward and one step back; however, from this new perspective Roy understood that this is what teaching and learning looks like. He found the most important moments were the one-step-back moments (in which Roy maintained his emotional balance, regardless of Matt's behaviour) and one-to-one emotional connection-building, and did not place any blame or shame on himself. It was in these moments that Roy supported Matt to break the previous negative-behaviour cycle. Matt was learning that his needs were now met more quickly when he allowed Roy to support him. He was feeling more emotionally safe about that, rather than feeling emotionally safe in knowing how his teacher used to respond to his rudeness. As Matt witnessed his teacher maintaining his sense of calm despite his surface behaviour, and discovered that Roy still happily met with him one to one during the school day, he learned that it was also safe for him to feel such emotions and tip the scales.

THE FIVE CS

Beliefs are just thoughts that we keep thinking about in the same way. If we want to change our perception as an initial step in behaviour support, we need to practise changing our thoughts. You might prefer to first practise the Five Cs as a reflective exercise after the event (so, after an interaction with a child in your care). Initially it may be difficult to do in the moment and that is OK (no blame, no shame).

- **Communication.** The child/young person's behaviour is communicating a need for emotional connection.
- **Calm.** This moment is a teaching and learning opportunity.
- **Curious.** What feeling is my child seeking?
- **Connect.** How can I meet their emotional needs?
- **Convey.** What does my behaviour look like in this moment from the child's perspective?

I come back to the Five Cs throughout the book, and build on them to tailor them to specific situations. Revisit the Five Cs on this page as often as you'd like, or any time you need a refresher. It's important to grasp these before progressing on to extended versions you'll come to later on.

From good to better

People often think of behaviour modification as a sudden or big, tangible event, but it doesn't have to be. Changing our perception is one of the most empowering and effective initial steps in behaviour support. We have the power to change our minds. If we have thought in one way for a while, it's OK to change our thoughts and have flexibility of perception. If we want our children to think and then behave differently, we must also be able to do the same. If we focus on problems, we *will* see problems everywhere and in everything. Shifting perspective and reframing each and every undesirable behaviour moment as a teaching and learning opportunity immediately changes our perception of the event. We can then begin to see improvements immediately, as the hardest part of behaviour support tends to be the way it makes us feel.

So now, if we can practise thinking about the situation and the behaviour as part of a child or young person's growth, we can feel differently about it. It will, of course, be different for every child, as they all seek emotional connection in different ways and for different reasons. However, every child needs to be supported from the perspective that they are already good enough and we're just helping them to do even better. You are not going from bad to good – instead perceive it as good to better. There is *always* something positive in every single young person.

CHAPTER 1 ROUND-UP

- We can all look at the exact same behaviour or scenario but perceive it differently.

- Negative emotions can manifest as negative behaviours.

- Undesirable behaviours tell us that there is a need to emotionally balance.

- Children need to feel seen, heard and safe.

- Children learn more from what they see than what they hear.

- Behaviour support begins with a mindset and not a list of strategies.

Gentle Guidance

What to do when the adults don't agree

It's not unusual for adults to have different ideas on how best to support a child – parents (whether separated or together), teachers, carers or people in other key support roles will often vary in opinion. Everyone's perception is right to them, so trying to get other adults to agree that your way is better may be an uphill struggle. Instead, start by trying to understand why they hold the perceptions they do and where they've come from (for example, their own upbringing or other past experiences). Once you open your mind to differing perceptions and why they exist, you are better placed to be able to consider if there are any opinions you do agree with. If you're really struggling, begin by establishing this goal (which should be common to everyone): that the child in question needs emotional certainty, safety, security and support, which can be achieved through establishing routines, boundaries, expectations and considered language. If adults are doing different things within these areas, that's OK and the child can still progress. If not, rest assured that's also OK; focus on what you have control over. Gentle guidance, if implemented consistently, is impactful enough that you will see increments of progress from young people, regardless of what other adults are doing (or not doing).

The upcoming suggestions are covered in more detail throughout the book: follow the page references to learn more. I would suggest reading the book in full first and then coming back to put this gentle guidance into practice.

Routines and **language:** Routines and considered language provide children with emotional certainty and emotional support. By creating daily routines *with* the young person, this means that even if their routine is different elsewhere, they're still receiving emotional certainty. Two consistent routines, albeit different, is best, but rest assured, one consistent routine is better than none. Allow them to be part of the routine expectations by using the language of choice (page 220) to provide them with safe control (page 101).

Rewards and **effects:** For emotional clarity and stability, in feel-good moments discuss *what happens if…* with a young person, that is, any 'effects' (or what others might call 'consequences') in the event they overstep the pre-agreed boundary or expectation. Allow them to be part of the decision-making by using the language of choice (page 220). Again, this may vary in two different environments, but consistency within each environment is the key factor, or at least in one if this can't be achieved in both.

Boundaries and **expectations** (page 217)**:** These provide emotional safety and security. Support the young person to understand the boundary and to meet the expectation. This can be via explaining the purpose of the boundary and expectation, with a visual timetable that reflects the pre-agreed routine (even if, in different environments, the timetables differ slightly).

Emotional connection (page 128): This element is what will support the young person the most if there are inconsistencies between adults with the implementation of the previous points.

Thought–Feeling–Action

Imagine being in a helicopter, looking down at hundreds of cars below. From that perspective high in the sky, the lines of vehicles look beautiful against the green fields surrounding the many roads. You can see the entire landscape and think to yourself that the cars are just a part of the bigger picture, adding to its beauty. These thoughts help you feel at peace – happy and grateful for the helicopter ride, and these feelings lead you to thank the pilot for such an amazing experience.

Next, imagine you are in one of those cars on the ground. All you can see ahead of you is a long line of vehicles in a sea of traffic and the very last thing on your mind is how beautiful it is! In fact, you can't comprehend how in this moment anyone could describe this traffic as beautiful. From this perspective you feel as if you'll be in it for ever without an end in sight. You feel frustrated and short-tempered and when a driver tries to cut in front of you, you shout, 'How dare you? What's special about you? Get in line like the rest of us!'

Whatever your role is in the lives of the children you care for, when you're in the thick of it, like being in the traffic, it can often feel endless and as if there is no hope. It's totally understand-able for that to be your perception from where you are at that moment, and it can feel very intense when you are so close to the perceived problems.

Case study

Alec, who was twelve, soon to be thirteen, was refusing to follow instructions from his father, Craig. In the moments when Alec was refusing to comply and being oppositional and confrontational, Craig felt as if he'd lost control; he was exasperated and even embarrassed.

I started working with Craig, encouraging him to take a few steps back and look at the entire landscape, the whole of his child. He still saw the perceived problems, but he could also see his son's charm, his strength and determination, and when seeing those aspects, Craig could see it differently from this perspective. In this way, Alec, who was refusing to follow instructions and do as he'd been asked, was now seen by his dad as strong and independent. This made him think, *I wonder why he doesn't want to do it my way?* and, *Does Alec have another, even better way of doing it? How can I nurture this trait so that he can become a leader? Not being a follower will be a real strength and of great benefit to him in life. I want to support him to utilise this strength in a more desirable way.*

Our perceptions link directly to our thought, feelings and actions (for more information on the neuroscience behind this, look up the 'cognitive triangle' online for more information). As we saw above, there's no one truth in whether the traffic was beautiful or not, only two different perspectives, equally valid and understandable in their own right. Exactly the same applies to behaviour. Whether it's two parents, other family members, professionals, or adult and child – everyone perceives things differently and most believe that their perception is the right one!

I'm not here to tell you what's right or wrong with regard to behaviour: that would, in fact, be in conflict with my whole approach. I'm here to encourage you, as you support a young person, to be consciously aware of differing perceptions and how they directly impact on our individual thoughts, feelings and actions. If we accept that there are different perspectives, we open ourselves up to more options, which can lead to more resolutions. This also allows us to see how and why in a moment someone else may perceive something differently, the most important 'someone' being the child. Once we can 'see' from this standpoint, the way we think, feel and respond to the behaviour can be entirely different, creating a different mirror effect that benefits both the young person and yourself. In Chapter 10, I include a resource to help you identify your thought–feeling–action cycle (page 234).

Accept all feelings

It's not wrong for a child to feel what they feel. As the adults supporting them, we just want the action not to be undesirable when they feel a certain way. Remember, our aim shouldn't be a desire to exert control over the young people in our lives. If you do find this to be the case, gently ask yourself, without any blame or shame, why that may be. Exploring our own beliefs is OK – it's all part of the process – but if it doesn't feel accessible or comfortable right now to take a closer look at your own behaviours, that's OK too, you can set this book down and revisit it when you are ready.

At the time of writing this book, both of my children are teenagers and I've been working in education supporting young people for twenty years. Despite this, I can honestly and happily say that I don't know all there is to know about education or children. I absolutely love expanding my knowledge, learning and working collaboratively with others. I don't get everything 'right' all the time and there is no blame or shame in that. I want the children in my care to know this and to see this in me. Feelings of guilt, shame or failure do not serve us. From a place of such feelings, how can we teach children that it's OK to make mistakes, to change our minds, to change the way in which things are done, and so on?

Coping mechanisms

It's very empowering to be free of judgement, but I didn't always feel this liberated. From as young as I can remember, I wanted everything to be 'perfect'. I recall tidying up my room 'perfectly' and then saying out loud the phrase 'starting from now'. What I meant was that everything was perfectly neat and tidy and from that moment on I'd maintain the feeling of everything being in its place, this fleeting feeling of 'perfection'. I know now looking back that this was simply a coping mechanism. When I **thought** about the abuse I was enduring, it made me **feel** very much out of control and emotionally unsafe, so my **action** was to create a perfect environment that then made me feel momentarily safe and in control of something. Children and the adults they become will all develop their own coping mechanisms, some more out in the open, and others more hidden, like mine. Our individual thought processes and circumstances will manifest as different behaviours; for some it may be nail-biting if certain thoughts make them feel anxious, for example, or hair-twirling, talking too much or becoming lost for words altogether. Others might become frustrated quickly or short-tempered, or find something to complain about that can take attention away from an uncomfortable feeling, or be used as a vehicle to express pent-up emotions.

Thought–feeling–action cycles

Case study

Many years ago I worked in a school with a teacher colleague called Lia. When she **thought** life was going OK and she was **feeling** good, her **action** was that she was really great with the children. She was funny and charismatic and if a child was displaying undesirable behaviours, she was able to support them through it without becoming unstable herself. When she was in a positive thought–feeling–action cycle she could see the entire landscape of the child, like being in the helicopter.

I remember that Lia worked particularly well with a student named Sophie. At times Sophie believed that she wasn't as well liked by teachers as other pupils, which led her to think that she wasn't as clever or capable in her schoolwork, meaning she referred to herself as 'dumb' or 'stupid'. Lia understood from Sophie's perspective that in certain moments Sophie's perception impacted on her thoughts and feelings, which then manifested as undesirable behaviours. Although the behaviour still affected Lia, and she would rather Sophie's emotions weren't expressed in particular ways, such as being verbally aggressive towards herself and other children, she didn't feel overwhelmed by it or as if there was no end (like being stuck in the traffic from an on-the-ground perspective). Lia remembered and could still see, even when Sophie shouted at her to go away and that she hated her, that she could focus on the child behind the behaviour — Sophie was a caring and loving girl, with a real talent for art and so much potential.

When Lia's personal life went through a difficult patch, though, so too did her dynamic with Sophie. Lia's marriage was ending, which was understandably a very tumultuous time, and in the roughly eighteen months prior to her husband leaving, she was under a lot of strain. Leading up to their marriage ending, there were times when she would come to work with **thoughts** about a disagreement at home the night before leaving her **feeling** low, confused and emotionally drained. When she came into school and Sophie was displaying undesirable behaviours, all Lia could see (and therefore respond to) was what was right in front of her. Everywhere she looked, there was a problem, just like being in the worst traffic jam with no exits for miles ahead. Her **action** on these days was to snap at the other children in the class, 'You're all too noisy today!' She'd tell me that 'the school building feels too stuffy today', she'd confide in colleagues that, 'Mr Levi was so rude to me today,' and so on. Of course, to Sophie her voice became ever so slightly louder, her body language a little bit more rigid, her facial expressions that much sterner and, overall, her patience ran out much more quickly.

Lia's way of coping with how she was feeling was to express pent-up emotions as complaints, because sub-consciously that felt better and safer to her than breaking down in floods of tears at work. We all have different coping-mechanism actions, and there is no blame or shame in it once we understand this from the perspective that we're just trying to cope. What is important however, is that we move past the coping stage, firstly by having *conscious* awareness (particu-larly as 93 per cent of our communications are subconscious – more on this later). Furthermore, we need to understand the power of our thoughts and how they impact our feelings and actions. From here we can then practise different ways to respond when we hold particular thoughts and feelings, such as adopting a helicopter perspective when circum-stances arise.

Have a think about what your coping-strategy actions are. You may not know straight away, and it may take a while to recognise them consciously, so take your time in the upcoming weeks and reveal to yourself how you cope with uncomfortable thoughts and feelings. How do you act or react from an on-the-ground, in-traffic perspective? And remember, no blame, no shame. When I spoke with Lia, she initially strongly denied it all and said that she would never let anything outside of work interfere with work. However, once reassured by 'no blame, no shame', she opened up to me and could see from Sophie and other colleagues' perspectives that her thoughts and feelings were having a subtle impact on her actions. This was enough for them to be sensed by Sophie and others, which created a mirror effect, and of course those days were always the hardest for both Lia and Sophie.

Having this awareness of our thought–feeling–action cycle can be very empowering because it gives us a better understanding of how we might support a child more effectively. It reminds us of the mirror effect and how those around us (adults and children) are often more perceptive and sensitive to our state of mind than we may imagine. It doesn't mean we'll never bring our problems to work or let something challenging happening in one part of our lives affect another part (we're not robots) – life is going to throw us some curveballs, after all. On page 116, we look at why *you* feeling supported is key when helping to meet the emotional needs of others.

Progression, not perfection

Following my conversation with Lia, she at first became quite frustrated with herself when reflecting on a day when she was in a negative thought–feeling–action cycle. She found it difficult to emotionally stabilise Sophie when she was feeling unstable herself. She was seeking perfection (just as I was when I was younger with my room-tidying), and so was always disappointed, because life isn't perfect and never will be – and that's OK! I've had to learn via the rollercoaster of life, which looks different for us all, how to stabilise myself and not be negatively influenced by others. I'm still learning and forever will be. It may help when practising this perspective in or after a 'moment' dealing with a child, to tell yourself: *I seek progression, not perfection.* This mantra, just like when we can understand different perspectives, along with where and why people may hold the beliefs that they do (refer to Chapter 1), can immediately change our thoughts, feelings and actions. If we can perceive life as progressive and learn to be OK when others are not, then we practise a helicopter perspective more often than not.

Lia continuously told herself 'no blame, no shame', and by aiming for progression instead of perfection she began to adopt a consistent helicopter perspective that was beneficial to both herself and the young people she supported.

The bigger picture

As a teacher, my favourite subject to teach (and learn myself) is maths. From the national curriculum in England, in the mathematics programmes of study, key stages 1 and 2, the purpose of study states that:

> Mathematics is a creative and highly interconnected
> discipline ... A high-quality mathematics education
> therefore provides a foundation for understanding the
> world ... mathematics is an interconnected subject
> in which pupils need to be able to move fluently
> between representations of mathematical ideas ...
> The expectation is that the majority of pupils will move
> through the programmes of study at broadly the same
> pace. However, decisions about when to progress should
> always be based on the security of pupils' understanding
> and their readiness to progress to the next stage ...
> Those who are not sufficiently fluent with earlier material

*should consolidate their understanding, including
through additional practice, before moving on.*[*]

When it comes to academic study, we can readily adopt a helicopter perspective to see the bigger picture. We understand and accept the need to learn fundamental maths skills in order to become competent in the subject area. In school the interconnected maths curriculum repeats core skills year upon year to support pupils to embed knowledge and understanding. However, it doesn't always occur to us that we need to train our brain in the same way to learn behaviour skills (even though our brain is a complex organ that controls thought, memory, emotion and every process that regulates our body — far more complex than the maths curriculum). Our brains automatically send out and receive chemical and electrical signals throughout the body and billions of nerve cells that coordinate thought, emotion, behaviour, movement and sensation. While all the parts of our brain work together, each part is responsible for a specific function — controlling everything from our heart rate to our mood. It's important to note here that for some people, there can be alterations in the brain that impact on individual perception. For example, trauma can affect the shape of the brain and certain conditions such as ADHD can mean brain make-up is different. Regardless of any differences in the brain, the in-the-moment as well as pre-emptive tools in this book are universal, helping to reduce the risk of particular behaviours reoccurring in the same way.

_____

[*] Mathematics programmes of study: key stages 1 and 2, National curriculum in England, 2013, https://assets.publishing.service.gov.uk/government/uploads/system/uploads/attachment_data/file/335158/PRIMARY_national_curriculum_-_Mathematics_220714.pdf

Behaviour building blocks

So why is it harder to adopt a helicopter perspective with regard to the learning and development of behaviour? Most often the answer is because of how it makes us *feel*. If our children are struggling with grasping a maths concept at school, it's unlikely to make us feel ashamed, embarrassed, overwhelmed, scared or deskilled. Generally our thought–feeling–action process may be similar to the following:

Thought: *They may need some extra support/practice, or they will get it in time, or I might not be able to assist them but I'll find out who can, or I remember when I found that difficult as a child.*

Feeling: *Understanding, patience, calm, hopefulness.*

Action: *Encouraging/supportive language, seek additional support/advice, soothe and comfort.*

However, if a child is struggling with their behaviour, generally our thought–feeling–action process may be similar to the following:

Thought: *What will others think about me/my child? or Will this ever get better? or Does this mean I am not a good parent/practitioner? or I need to 'fight' for them, or I don't know what to do.*

Feeling: *Failure, upset, anxiousness, overwhelm, impatience, frustration, anger, loss of control.*

Action: *Reprimand, retreat, shut down, cry, shout, blame, attack, compliance.*

Continuing with maths as an analogy, looking again at the wording from the National Curriculum, let's see how we might successfully teach children and young people core, fundamental life skills:

Mathematics is a creative and highly interconnected discipline. Each year of maths in school builds on prior knowledge and skills to learn new knowledge and skills. If you are not fluent in your times tables, for example, it may be difficult to learn and understand fractions and ratios later on. It's all interconnected and children will learn at different rates, in different ways, for different reasons. When children are struggling, we see an opportunity to teach and learn. We support them via repetition, consistency, practice and allowing years for them to make and rectify mistakes. This process allows children to feel that there are choices and options to succeed, and the support provided, via modelling, resources, patience and understanding, helps them to feel in control, safe in the knowledge that everything will be OK.

From a similar perspective, let's look at behaviour:

Behaviour is creative and highly interconnected. Each year in a child's life builds upon prior knowledge and skills to learn new knowledge and skills. If you are still learning how to share or take turns, for example, it may be difficult when starting school to share with the other children in the classroom, or know how and when to wait your turn in the playground. It is all interconnected and children will learn at different rates, in different ways, for different reasons. When children are struggling we should see this as an opportunity to teach and learn. We can support them via repetition, consistency, practice and allowing *years*, if need be, to make and rectify mistakes. Children will then feel that there are choices and options to succeed, no matter what the circumstances, and the support provided via modelling, resources, patience and understanding will help them to feel in control, safe in the knowledge that everything will be OK.

How did you feel reading the last paragraph on behaviour? You're likely to have fully understood the words. You may have **thought** that the maths analogy is logical and makes sense when thinking about behaviour. The **feeling** of pressure with regard to time or feelings of frustration or anger are likely to be almost non-existent when we perceive our child's behaviour from the wider helicopter perspective. Knowing and allowing for years, if need be, means that our **action** or reactions in response to certain behaviours drastically change. No matter the age of the young person, if we adopt a similar helicopter perspective to behaviour, it will have a direct and positive impact on our thoughts, feelings and actions, similar to if they were struggling with a maths concept.

How to take a step back

It's all well and good me telling you to observe your child in the bigger picture, but it can be hard to know how to actually go about doing so. I often work with parents and teachers showing them how to adopt the helicopter approach, as it's such an effective tool for sustainable behaviour support. Coming up is a step-by-step exercise to help adapt your mindset to look at the bigger picture, allowing you to see there's more than one way to view a situation – please note that this takes continual practice until it becomes second nature. For some, depending on where you are currently, this may take a few weeks and for others a few months, so no blame, no shame; it is all part of the process. I want this exercise to show you that behaviour support really does begin as a mindset – a crucial first step and the integral aspect many people miss or skip. Without questioning and shaping our mindset, the practical strategies we try to implement will not work long term.

THE FIVE STEPS

STEP 1: PERSPECTIVE

Practise considering the below questions as often as you can, in as many different scenarios as possible. The idea behind this is to remind yourself that everyone perceives a situation differently.

Ask yourself, another adult or the child, where appropriate, why you hold the beliefs that you/they do from your/their perspectives. What's your view on X? What do you think about Y? How do you feel about that? Why? *Practise, practise, practise.*

For example, imagine two parents hold opposing views on whether their baby should use a dummy. Instead of launching into an argument about it, they make a concerted effort to find out why they hold the views they do. Each asks the other about their childhood experiences of dummies and any other relevant information about why they feel strongly about them. Similarly, a parent and their teenager might disagree on how much screen time the young person should have. Ideally they'd have an open conversation about this, discussing the whys behind their opinions, which for the parents might include how different (for better or worse) their childhood was compared to their child's and how their past informs their current viewpoint. You don't necessarily need to come to an agreement with another perspective, or a resolution; it's more a case that understanding another point of view can immediately change how you feel about a situation or even a person.

(**Note:** When you're asking a child these questions, only do so when they are feeling good and *not* in moments of distress!)

STEP 2: COMMUNICATION

Practise the thought that *all* behaviour is a manifestation or communication of emotion, no matter how undesirable the surface behaviour may be.

Consider the whys behind the behaviour. Is the child anxious, fearful, feeling out of control, unworthy, and so on? Actively think what the reason could be. What may they be trying to communicate via their behaviour in this moment? *Practise, practise, practise.*

(**Note:** If you're not sure of the 'why' behind the behaviour, you can fall back on it being that all children want to be seen, heard and to feel safe – it will fall into at least one of these categories.)

STEP 3: UNDERSTANDING

Understand how positive and negative thought–feeling–action cycles affect your life experiences.

Ask yourself: What perspective do I have in this current moment? Is it a helicopter or an on-the-ground, in-traffic perspective? What coping mechanism actions do I adopt when I feel uncomfortable? *Practise, practise, practise.*

(**Note**: remember to be mindful of the mirror effect and how we impact each other, when in a positive or negative cycle.)

STEP 4: PROGRESSION

Continually tell yourself *no blame, no shame*, until you believe it.

Remind yourself, *I seek progression and not perfection. Practise, practise, practise.*

(**Note**: this will be for ever! While you will get used to and eventually embody these beliefs, life will happen around you and progression is continuous. There is no end. Learn to be OK with and eventually excited about continual growth.)

STEP 5: CONNECTION

Find a way to emotionally connect daily with your child or children.

Use the scales illustration resource (page 31) and maintain your stability throughout. *Practise, practise, practise.*

(**Note:** it may take weeks, months or years to balance or tip the scales, depending on the child and their circumstances, but they *will* make progress.)

As we progress through the book, these Five Steps should be practised over and over again, as they'll give you the foundations to successfully implement all the other strategies we'll come to later on. Think of these Five Steps as pre-strategies that encourage the mindset needed for the strategies to be successful. I can't promise a quick fix, but I can guarantee that there will be incremental progress (which we will explore next). There is no regression and only progression if we maintain the mindset, and how exciting and empowering is that?

Adjusting our mindset

Case study

Anna's teenage son Max was what she described as a bright child with a poor attitude at times. She told me that she was tired of constantly having to tell him off about the same things over and over, and she wanted him to show her more respect. As I got to know Anna, she explained to me that, as a child, her parents didn't always understand where she was coming from, so she wanted to parent Max differently, specifically for him to feel that he could speak to her about anything. Respect was also very important to her, and from her perspective, she believed that meant a child not talking rudely or answering back to their parents — which Max sometimes did. While she didn't always feel like her parents 'got' her, she did respect them by not answering back. It was obvious that Anna and Max had become stuck in their own thought–feeling–action cycles:

Anna

Thought: I can't believe he's disrespected me by answering back — he just doesn't listen!

Feeling: Upset, angry, frustrated, impatient, exasperated, tense, loss of control.

Action: Confiscating Max's phone, stern/raised voice, distressed facial expressions.

Max

Thought: I can't believe she has no respect for me by not allowing me to express how I feel — she doesn't listen!

Feeling: Upset, angry, frustrated, impatient, exasperated, tense, loss of control.

Action: Confrontational tone, stern/raised voice, distressed facial expressions.

Both Anna and Max were operating from their own belief systems. Anna's view on respect from child to adult was, *Please listen to me, I am the adult and only wanting what's best for you. Can you not understand and see it from my point of view?*

Max's view on respect from child to adult was, *How can you know what's best for me if you can't see it from my point of view? You keep talking about respect but don't show me any!*

There's also the mirror effect at play here, as described in the previous chapter. Anna's intentions were coming from a good place, but from Max's perspective he was finding it difficult to believe in his mum's words or receive the support she so desperately wanted to give him. This was because her action and reaction, due to her thoughts and feelings, appeared in opposition. Max was learning in this moment far more from his mum's actions than her words, and so mirrored behaviours back to her, which kept them stuck in their cycles.

In order to break the negative thought—feeling—action cycle, Anna began to practise the Five Steps. She began to practise thoughts that Max might perceive things differently from her. Although she also did that as a teenager, she didn't answer her parents back, but she remembered what it felt like in those moments. She also began to practise the thought that all behaviour is a communication and considered, *Why is Max behaving in this way, what are his needs, how does he feel?* Over time, the more that Anna practised these thoughts, the calmer she felt. She practised her understanding of their individual thought—feeling—action cycles and continually asked herself, *Do I have a helicopter or an on-the-ground in-traffic perspective?* She began to feel more patient with Max, even when he was becoming impatient, sometimes talking over her, but in those moments she was consistent in her approach, as she now perceived it as an opportunity to teach and learn via the mirror effect. She was conscious that if she wanted him to be patient, her own action would need to be one of patience, and sometimes she demonstrated this better than at other times. However, Anna did not blame or shame herself; instead she said openly to Max, 'I became impatient again and I apologise, I'm learning too and it's OK to make and rectify mistakes.'

In doing this, Max's respect for his mum began to grow immensely and he was able to much better receive the support and advice that she was providing for him. He also then wanted to respond and interact (where he didn't before), when his mum emotionally connected with him daily, which for them was by cooking together (one of Max's passions). Through this process Anna began to feel hopeful that all would be OK. She no longer needed Max to share the exact same perspective as her and did not feel like she was losing control if he didn't. She was learning not to be dependent on Max acting in the exact way that she wanted him to in order to feel better. This allowed Anna to become mindful of any concern over Max leading her to becoming controlling, and this awareness meant she didn't fall into the habit of ruling and parenting through fear, which had been a tendency before.

A flexible mindset helps us to be more consciously aware of not holding the children in our care responsible for how we feel. It allows us to remain steady in the face of adversity without any need to be dependent on controlling external conditions in order to feel good, or needing others to behave a certain way in order to feel better. We can't control others, but we can control our responses to them, and the good news is we can change our mindset to have a more positive impact on our thought–feeling–action cycle.

TRY IT: *For one week if you find yourself in a situation with a child behaving in an undesirable way, ask yourself,* Am I steady in this moment? *Then actively and mindfully change your action to ensure that you remain steady, positive and happy.*

Tipping the scale

When learning a new skill or concept, we don't go from not knowing to knowing in one jump. I didn't expect to know all I would have learned by the end of my four-year degree during my second month at university! The same goes for when I learned to drive, ride a bike, swim, and raise and teach children.

We don't go from undesirable to desirable, from not able to able in a single leap. There are many increments of progress to be recognised and celebrated along the way. Often the feelings of pressure, failure and overwhelm come from an expectation that if one side of the scale is heavy with undesirable behaviours, we must find ways to immediately balance it as quickly as possible. But to level up takes time, and the recognition and celebration of progress along the way keeps both us and the children that we are supporting feeling good enough to keep going.

Increments of progress

There have been frequent times writing this book where I've had to adopt my own strategies and practise what I preach. As you know, my mum has dementia, and when she was first diagnosed, she lived alone without any carers or cameras in place to ensure her safety and support her care. Nearly five years on, Mum lives with us and we have morning carers seven days a week and a carer who comes for four hours a day, four times a week. As explained earlier, my mum's dementia is fairly aggressive, and she requires continuous care throughout the day and can't be left alone for more than about twenty minutes. Though we all love being in a position to care for my mum, it can also be draining, especially combined with raising two teenagers, as well as the typical day-to-day hubbub of work and life.

Today was an especially difficult day. Mum has just started to wake up at night and walk up and down for hours, and so she's exhausted during the day. When she's tired, everything becomes ten times more confusing and these confused thoughts lead to distressed feelings that manifest as behaviours such as crying, shouting, refusal and aggression. Remember we can't control others' behaviour but we can control our responses to it. Most days, I do successfully manage to practise what I preach, and regardless of how my mum is behaving that day, I'm more often than not able to maintain a helicopter perspective. So, after a tough day today, I consciously took a step back as I noted and appreciated the incremental progress that has been made to date.

We used to have no carer support and although we still do not have full-time care, we have more hours of support than we used to. *That's progress.* I used to have no idea of what to do when my mum was emotionally unstable, so I'd go up and down with her emotionally. Now, even though some days I still feel overwhelmed and sad that the mum I used to know is fading away, I'm consciously aware of my thought–feeling–action patterns, so when they're occasionally negative, I don't place any blame or shame on myself. *That's progress.* I used to feel so frustrated when others commented, 'She seems fine to me!' whereas now when someone makes a similar comment, I fully understand that from their perspective she probably does, in the fleeting moments they're with her. *That's progress.*

In moments of self-doubt I adopt a helicopter perspective and celebrate the incremental progress to date; doing so helps me to quickly stabilise. If I had allowed thoughts such as, *How will we cope in the upcoming months if she continues to deteriorate at this rate?* to take over, I'd have had an on-the-ground in-the-traffic perspective. I might have felt heavy feelings of fear and worry, and my action when Mum was being aggressive might have been to become frustrated or tearful. I know this because this still happens on occasion and that's absolutely fine. It's fine because I can reflect afterwards and understand why I felt as I did, which is more often than not due to tiredness or not looking after myself properly.

Get to know your own thought–feeling–action cycles and where those initial thoughts originate from and why (we'll explore this more later in the book). There really is no right or wrong, just different perspectives, depending on your thought, feeling and action, but we have choices, and the more we practise the uplifting perspective, the more empowered we feel and the better positioned we are to support others' behaviour.

Acknowledging and celebrating incremental progress is a game changer because not only will you feel good in the moment, it'll spur you on, too. You can literally go from feeling like you're crawling through traffic to soaring high in the air. If you practise it consistently, the impact it has on the children in your care over time is amazing.

Support, acknowledge, celebrate

Case study

Stella was in her second year of teaching. She was doing a wonderful job and asked me for some advice with a pupil, Sajid, who would become distraught when she marked his work with a pink pen (pink meant that the answer was incorrect; the green pen meant that the answer was correct). Sajid had additional needs and his needs were impacting powerfully on how he perceived not only himself but also those around him. I asked Stella how she viewed Sajid's potential thought–feeling–action each time his book was marked. She said that she suspected Sajid thought he wasn't as clever as his peers (a perception he would often verbalise). Stella then went on to conclude that Sajid most likely felt embarrassed at times, frustrated and annoyed. This was having a direct impact on his actions, which were usually to refuse to do any more work, put his head down on the table and refuse to interact with anyone, or cry, or shout for everyone to leave him alone.

From Sajid's perspective on his schoolwork, he was either doing well (green pen) or not doing well (pink pen). There was no opportunity for him to see, feel or understand the increments of progress. To help track his increments of progress, we introduced a number of other coloured pens to support Sajid – in fact, Stella used it with the entire class. The system became: pink indicated the child had not yet grasped the concept, blue meant they'd begun to understand, orange meant that they strongly understood the concept but not fully, and *then* green meant it was fully understood. They could all now see how they were progressing and Sajid's increments of progress were celebrated with him. Stella also spoke to her colleagues regularly about Sajid's increments of progress to remind herself that progress was continually being made, even on the days that he occasionally refused to do any more work, put his head down on the table, cried or shouted.

There are many other ways that we can **first support** and **then acknowledge** and **celebrate** young people's increments of progress, and below are a couple of examples:

Case study

Toddler Joanna was repeatedly throwing herself on the floor and screaming when it was time to tidy her toys away and get ready for bed.

Incremental progress support

Visual support with a picture timetable to aid Joanna in the transition from playing, to tidying up, to putting her pyjamas on.

Emotional support for Joanna by labelling her feelings: 'I can see that you're crying and it's OK to be sad that it's time to stop playing now.'

Language support using the language of choice: 'Would you like to put the toy in that box or this one?' or 'When we go upstairs, would you like to wear your green or blue pyjamas?'

Providing children with boundaried choices and safe control helps them feel empowered. If we limit or eliminate young people's choice and control, they will seek it in other, more undesirable ways.

Acknowledge and celebrate the increments of progress

- Joanna less frequently throws herself on the floor and screams when it's time to tidy her toys away and get ready for bed. *Acknowledge and celebrate.*

  It *is* progress that the frequency is less, even if she is still throwing herself on the floor and the screaming remains the same.

- Joanna no longer throws herself on the floor, but still screams when it's time to tidy her toys away and get ready for bed. *Acknowledge and celebrate.*

  It *is* progress that she no longer throws herself on the floor, even though she is still screaming at high volume!

- Joanna no longer screams but sobs loudly when it's time to tidy her toys away and get ready for bed. *Acknowledge and celebrate.*

  It *is* OK that she is sobbing loudly, as that is huge progress from the previous high-pitched screams.

- Joanna no longer sobs loudly but cries softly when it's time to tidy her toys away and get ready for bed. *Acknowledge and celebrate.*

  There has been significant progress, as Joanna is tidying her toys away and getting ready for bed. It's OK for her to be sad, her feelings are valid; it is the *action* of screaming and throwing herself on the floor that was supported to change when she feels sad.'

Hopefully, at this point in the book you can see why perspective is so important. If you have an in-the-traffic, on-the-ground perspective, you would most likely think, *There's been no progress, as Joanna still cries just as she did at the start of this process!* However, if you adopt a helicopter perspective, you would say, *There's been significant progress. Although Joanna still cries when it's time to get ready for bed, it's nothing like how it used to be when she was screaming and throwing herself on the floor. I can see real progression and feel confident that she will continue to progress!*

Case study

Teenager Liam was, as his dad described, continuously 'conveniently forgetting' to tidy his room, unpack the dishwasher and do the hoovering. When told to do so, he would stomp around in his bedroom, mumble under his breath and have an extremely hostile facial expression.

Incremental progress support

Empowerment and **purpose** of the task: 'Liam, by doing these things you are demonstrating that you are really responsible and trustworthy.'

Emotional support for Liam by acknowledging his feelings: 'I can see that you're not happy about doing these things and

I understand that it is not a priority to you, so thank you for your contributions.'

Language support using the language of choice: 'Would you like me to tell you what days to hoover, or would you like to choose the days?'

By providing children with reasons for how they positively impact/contribute to the bigger picture, it gives them a sense of purpose.

Acknowledge and celebrate the increments of progress

- Liam, after deciding to choose which days to tidy his bedroom, hoover and unpack the dishwasher, initially throws his clothing from the floor and onto the bed, then into the wardrobe, reluctantly hoovers with a hostile facial expression and completely forgets to unpack the dishwasher. *Acknowledge and celebrate.*
  It *is* progress that he is doing more than he used to – which had been nothing!

- Liam still throws his clothing onto the floor and bed, then into the wardrobe, and reluctantly hoovers and unpacks the dishwasher with a hostile facial expression. *Acknowledge and celebrate.*
  It *is* progress that he's now completing all three tasks.

- Liam hangs some items of clothing on a hanger and throws the rest into the wardrobe. He reluctantly hoovers and unpacks the dishwasher, but no longer with a hostile facial expression. *Acknowledge and celebrate.*

It *is* progress that he is hanging up some clothes, whereas before it was none, and although still reluctant to hoover and unpack the dishwasher, his facial expression is no longer hostile.

- Liam hangs most items of clothing on a hanger in the wardrobe and reluctantly hoovers and unpacks the dishwasher. *Acknowledge and celebrate.*

  It *is* progress that he's now hanging up most of his clothes, most of the time, and although still reluctant to hoover and unpack the dishwasher, he is doing so consistently with a reminder on occasion.

Young people need to feel that there is a purpose. They need to understand the bigger picture and how they fit into it, and also feel that their thoughts and feelings are considered with regard to them having choices and safe control. If they do not feel that there is scope for them to be heard, they will often find their own, sometimes undesirable ways to make themselves seen, heard and feel safe and in control.

When supporting, acknowledging and celebrating the increments of progress, be mindful of the wider helicopter perspective. For some children, it will be weeks before we see progress in the way that we would like, while for others it will be months or even years. It's all OK, as each child is uniquely different, with different needs, and will develop at different rates, no matter what others their age may or may not be doing. This can, of course, be understandably frustrating. However, a helicopter perspective can and will support these frustrations.

THE FIVE CS FOR
THOUGHT–FEELING–ACTION

Here's an extended version of the Five Cs exercise from the previous chapter, which will help you practise the topics in this chapter. Please don't attempt this if you haven't yet practised and feel confident with the original (page 46). Take your time and do it properly (without blame or shame), no matter how long it takes, as it will be worthwhile in the end.

Communication. The child/young person's behaviour is communicating a need for emotional connection. *Ask why continuously – what are their needs?*

Calm. This moment is a teaching and learning opportunity. *Remain steady and 'be' the example.*

Curious. What feeling is my child seeking? *Label the feelings.*

Connect. How can I meet their emotional needs? *Language of choice.*

Convey. What does my behaviour look like in this moment from the child's perspective? *Support, acknowledge and celebrate the increments of progress.*

CHAPTER 2 ROUND-UP

- We can't control a child's behaviour, but we can control our responses to it.

- Practise adopting a wider helicopter perspective by repeating the Five Steps (page 66).

- Our thoughts, feelings and actions are all connected. How we think and feel affects our actions.

- Progress may take weeks, months or years – allow for mistakes.

- Children and young people are not responsible for how we feel. They need to feel that they have choices, control and purpose.

- Seek progression not perfection – support, acknowledge and celebrate the increments of progress.

Gentle Guidance

Cause and effect
(aka 'consequences' or 'punishments')

I changed my use of the word 'consequences' to 'effect' some time ago as there are so many strong negative connotations with 'consequences', and our perceptions of how they're enforced can vary quite a bit. My other issue with the traditional implementation of consequences is uncertainty around their effectiveness. Issuing consequences or doling out punishments doesn't necessarily mean that you won't see repeat behaviours if they're not coupled with an understanding of *why* a young person behaved as they did. They can also leave everyone (adult and child) feeling pretty resentful, which is not a great basis for fostering future cooperation. As we know, the best form of behaviour support is preventative and not reactive. Trying to implement strategies in an attempt to stop a behaviour in the moment often has limited effectiveness. Long-term sustainable behaviour support is when we look at the whys behind the behaviour and support the child from there.

The upcoming suggestions are covered in more detail throughout the book: follow the page references to learn more.

Routines and language: Creating daily routines with the child provides emotional certainty and emotional support. Invite their participation setting out their routine by using the language of choice (page 220) and providing them with safe control. This will

84

support them to express themselves and be an individual while still being part of the family, school and the wider community.

Boundaries and **expectations** (page 217): These provide emotional safety and security. Prepare the child when they are feeling good for what will happen if they don't adhere to the boundaries and expectations; for example, discuss with them any potential effects (or what others might call 'consequences'), such as needing to confiscate a digital device, or similar. Allow them to be part of the decision-making regarding *what happens if…* by using the language of choice (page 220). Making them aware in this way takes away or reduces any behaviours caused by shock and upset, should you issue an effect. Maintain consistency by referring to what you and the child have pre-agreed and don't be drawn into a long discussion about the effect, as it's been pre-agreed. You'll need to not be emotionally full (page 119) in order to do this!

Emotional support (page 111): Validate a young person's feelings using the 'seen, heard and safe' technique. When you validate feelings before reaffirming the boundary, over time the young person is able to accept the effect better. Offer comfort if you'd both like that, and ensure that you maintain the boundary (the pre-agreed effect of *what happens if…*).

Emotional connection (page 128): The attachment that you have with a young person (which can be achieved via emotional connection time) can make a huge difference in how they respond to an effect. You could potentially have a list of consequences that remain ineffective in practice if your attachment to them isn't strong.

Clearing the Fog: Behaviour as Communication

Have you ever felt so overwhelmed that you can't find the words to express it? Even when a caring friend or partner asks how you are, you feel so frazzled you don't even know where to start, how to unravel your emotions. Or you may have had a disconcerting feeling in the pit of your stomach you can't always explain, which gives you an unsettling feeling you can't shake.

There will be times when your child feels the same sense of overwhelm or distress – they may try to express this, but it isn't always easy for them. For a variety of reasons, it can be difficult for them to tell you with words how they are feeling, and sometimes they themselves don't even know what they are feeling precisely or how to describe it. When words fail them, or if they don't have the vocabulary to tell you, they will communicate through their behaviour (as do adults). It's our job as we support them to decode what they need and support them through it.

In the previous chapters, we looked at how a change in our perception creates new thoughts, feelings and actions, and having this viewpoint lets us understand that behaviour is a communication of need. When we think of a child's behaviour as communication, we can then begin to think from a clearer perspective about what they are trying to communicate (albeit in undesirable ways). They may, for example, be trying to say, 'I don't trust that you like me, as I don't much like myself,' or, 'Will you still be here for me if I continue to push you away?' or 'I don't know what else to do when I feel like this.' All of these examples (and there can be literally hundreds of different reasons) will make a child feel emotionally unsafe, insecure or unstable. These beliefs that form a young person's perceptions of the world and other people may have come from their attachment style (which we'll explore further in this chapter) and/or from trauma, a diagnosed or undiagnosed need, their age, or maybe they're just 'pushing it' by testing boundaries. It can become what I describe as a behaviour fog, where we're no longer sure where the behaviour originated or why, and therefore aren't sure what to do. Whatever the reasons behind the behaviour, every single young person wants and deserves to feel emotionally safe and it's why the behaviour-support strategies outlined in this chapter create a basis of support for all children that will help to clear the fog.

I hope these strategies show just how influential we are in a child's behaviour journey and how much we have the potential to gently guide them towards more desirable behaviours.

Seeing beyond the fog

In this example we see how strategies that encourage emotional security are always the most effective long term. When a child feels emotionally safe, this automatically aids in reducing anxiety and soothing stress. You'll also recognise some of the concepts from the first two chapters put into action here.

Case study

I worked with a family whose daughter, Haile, had a diagnosis of autism and sensory needs. Haile wasn't coping at school, and at home would frequently cause destruction, often breaking and damaging things like the TV or her parents' phones. Haile's parents were told by a well-meaning professional that this is what they'd have to get used to, as their child had special needs. They loved her dearly but had become somewhat fearful of her next outburst, so were appeasing her as best they could. They were understandably feeling very overwhelmed. I started to work with Haile's parents, offering them strategies to try to make life a bit less stressful for Haile and the whole family.

Firstly, we got to work on perception, as I wanted to support them to perceive Haile differently. Remember that mindset always comes before strategies – I knew that tackling their perception first would help them become more open-minded about trying a new range of support strategies. Their perceptions were that their daughter was disadvantaged due to her diagnosed needs and that her frequent moments of distress were evidence of how disadvantaged she was and how hard life would be for them all for ever more. They had little hope for her future. Due to these thoughts, the entire family lived in a state of high anxiety, dreading what might happen next. In turn, the parents' anxiety was being mirrored on a daily basis by Haile, and even though they would try to reassure her, 'It's OK, we're here and there's nothing to worry about,' Haile felt something very different from them, which heightened her own anxiety and so the cycle continued for years. No blame, no shame – from their perspective her parents always had done the very best for their daughter at each stage of her life. However, from a new perspective they could see it differently and so could try something different.

By practising the Five Steps (page 66) and becoming consciously aware of their own thoughts, feelings and actions, they were able to clear the fog and really see past how the situation was making them feel and how Haile might be perceiving them. Their perceptions changed from 'our daughter is disadvantaged due to her diagnosed needs' to 'our daughter has so many advantages by not being "the same" as her peers and her classmates'. From this clearer perspective, Haile's parents realised she shouldn't have to conform to what others perceived to be the norm. It also gave them the headspace to take a step back and look at her behaviour with a fresh pair of eyes. What had she been trying to tell them? Something that leapt out at them was how her sensory needs were being affected by both her home and school environments, and now that their perception was adjusted, they could see she'd been trying to communicate this via her behaviour. Every morning, Haile had been coming straight into the large, bright classroom from the large, loud playground. The same thing was happening on the transition from school to home – her sensory needs meant this was far too overstimulating and therefore distressing, and Haile was communicating via screaming and throwing objects. Behind her distress she was trying to say, 'This is all too much for me, please help me.'

In collaboration with the school, along with the other professionals who specialised in supporting autism and sensory needs, I arranged for Haile to have five minutes in a small, quiet space with a trusted adult before going into class in the morning. She'd later have five minutes in the alcove under the stairs (a small, safe space converted especially for her, which she loved) upon returning home from school. I wanted her to have the space to emotionally regulate before transitioning from one environment to the next. This was all put in place with clear routines that provided emotional certainty, expectations that provided emotional security, boundaries that provided emotional safety, and the language used by the adults around her that provided emotional support (we'll look at these in more detail later on).

This structure was very successful in stabilising Haile emotionally, and it was made possible by her parents' concerted and sustained effort to support her. Starting to be consciously aware that their own perceptions impacted directly on their thoughts, feelings and actions enabled them to clearly and consistently view their daughter's behaviour as a communication of need. This different approach helped them to clear the fog, allowing them to see what she really needed.

I'm happy to report that Haile is now in her twenties and successfully works with other families whose children have a diagnosis of autism.

The 'whys' behind the behaviour

There are so many reasons as to why a young person may be behaving as they are. It's important as we explore some of the reasons in this chapter that we remember whatever the underlying need(s), each and everyone has a right (and need) to feel seen, heard and safe. That's why offering strategies that support children in this way will help them regulate. Here's a reminder from earlier in the book of the need to balance the emotional scale.

Some children have additional communication and inter-action needs, sensory and/or physical needs, social, emotional and mental health needs, or cognition and learning needs, and some young people have experienced acute or chronic trauma. Depending on individual need, every child has a different perspective of the world and everything and everyone in it, resulting in different ways of communicating their needs and different rates of learning and development. Parents and other adults in supportive roles need to be responsible for seeking any additional or specialist support for the young people in their care and advocating for them. While the methods in this book will help to support children, be mindful that depending on individual need, some young people may require additional multi-agency support. Also keep in mind that there's no *one* right answer, no *one* right way of doing things, no *one* right way to live.

Attachment

As human beings, we all seek emotional connection and balance, but the way in which we seek it will vary from one individual to the next. Attachment theory is focused on the relationships and bonds between people. British psychologist John Bowlby was the first attachment theorist, describing attachment as a 'lasting psychological connectedness between human beings'. Bowlby observed that when children are anxious or scared, they will seek emotional connection from their primary caregiver(s), who in most instances are the child's parents. Bowlby believed that behaviours such as crying and screaming in children were evolutionary techniques designed to avoid separation from the primary caregiver, or used when reconnecting with a parent following separation. A child with a secure attachment style believes that the world is, generally, a safe place and that the people in it are also usually safe. They are comfortable receiving reassurance from their caregivers. Young people with an insecure attachment style (there are three insecure attachment styles or patterns of attachment) want and need reassurance from their caregivers, but often feel that they cannot depend on them. You'll likely find some push and pull with these young people – they want you due to their need for comfort but also push you away because of an underlying feeling of fear of rejection or abandonment.

If a child has an insecure attachment style, they may communicate their need for emotional connection by crying and screaming. For a school-aged child or adolescent we often find it difficult to see past these surface behaviours – such as verbal or physical aggression, inappropriate language, laughing and rudeness – because of how it makes us feel. With that in mind, it's important to maintain a helicopter perspective in order to perceive their behaviour as a communication of need. I know that's not always easy, especially when you feel very unsettled by certain behaviours, but it does get easier with practice.

Managing our feelings

Often when faced with undesirable surface behaviours, it's tempting to try to make the behaviour stop, or 'fix' it. It might cause us to freeze, fight back (mirroring their behaviours) or flee. It's less common to stay emotionally connected – to become curious rather than furious, understanding rather than demanding, to offer support instead of becoming distraught. As always, no blame, no shame – we're not all practised at sitting with uncomfortable feelings, and so we use coping strategies that interrupt the pain momentarily. However, just as with perceptions and thought–feeling–action, by reflecting on our own behaviour as communication and facing our feelings, we support young people to do the same, making it a teaching and learning opportunity.

When on the ground in the traffic, or in a 'moment' with a child or young person, it can be difficult to see past the fog that is their surface behaviour and identify the potential 'whys' causing them to behave in that particular way. It can be confusing, so it's vital for us to steady ourselves and assume a helicopter perspective in order to help clear the fog.

TRY IT: *The next time you are in a 'moment' with a child, use the Five Cs (page 46) to steady yourself, then ask yourself what they may be communicating to you via their behaviour – what are they trying to convey?*

Getting to the root of behaviour

Case study

Years ago, I worked with a young girl named Jamie, aged eleven, and her parents. They told me that Jamie would often cry and shout at them to go away when she was upset, but when they moved away, she followed them into the next room and continued to cry and shout! Jamie had a strong emotional bond with her parents (as her primary caregivers) and when she was anxious or scared, she would seek emotional connection with them. Her parents often felt anxious and scared too when faced with undesirable behaviour. They'd try to placate her by giving her what she was demanding, believing it would calm her down. On occasions it would calm her for a moment, but the same behaviours would resurface over and over again, so Jamie never appeared to be 'satisfied' for long. What appeared to be the 'reason' in any given moment for the undesirable behaviour (for example, her not wanting to eat the dinner her dad had prepared) was only the surface trigger and not the root cause.

Her parents were at a loss to know what to do for the best — they were in the thick of it, firefighting one stressful situation after the next. Without the benefit of a helicopter view, they were all stuck in negative thought–feeling–action cycles. Due to Jamie's parents' angst and worry, their responses were inconsistent and dependent on what mood Jamie was in that day — no blame, no shame. They were communicating back to their daughter emotional *imbalance*, as they responded to her behaviours by trying to appease her, and so Jamie mirrored inconsistent behaviours back to her parents.

When we first met, Jamie's parents told me how confused they were by her behaviour. They didn't know if it was happening due to her age, a potential undiagnosed need, or just her pushing the boundaries. My first port of call was to implement strategies (read on to see these) to clear the fog and that would support Jamie to feel seen, heard and safe. I knew that these strategies (no matter the 'whys') would help to reduce anxiety and relieve stress. They'd also clear the fog so that the adults around her could then more accurately assess any potential underlying root causes for her behaviour.

I'm still in touch with the family and Jamie is now in her late teens. I asked her, with the benefit of hindsight, what advice she'd give to parents and schoolteachers dealing with similar issues, and she told me, 'Please try to understand that every "I hate you" means "I need you" and every "go away" means "please stay".' I couldn't put it better myself!

Coming up are the strategies that helped Jamie's parents see beyond the fog to what Jamie was trying to communicate.

Become curious, not furious

As stated earlier, so often when faced with undesirable surface behaviours, we want to try and make the behaviour stop or 'fix' it because of how it makes us feel, be it uncomfortable, sad or concerned for the child, anxious or frustrated. This is a totally understandable response, but it doesn't get to the root cause of the issue.

The next time you're in a challenging situation with a child, one of the most effective first steps is to literally take a breath, which will calm your nervous system and help you steady yourself. From here you'll be better able to adopt a helicopter perspective, allowing you to take a step back and become curious (rather than furious) about the behaviour. As soon as you reframe the language to curious rather than furious, it immediately has a more positive impact on your thought, feeling and action. From this perspective you can now view the entire landscape. How might the child be perceiving things in this moment? For Jamie, she was in the traffic on the ground, and so from her perspective everything felt like a problem. Becoming rude and demanding was her way of coping with the uncomfortable feelings that she was experiencing. She felt out of control, so controlled her home environment via undesirable behaviours: *I may only feel good for a moment when I'm rude to Mum and Dad, but a moment of being in control, which avoids me feeling out of control, is better than feeling those other uncomfortable feelings.*

Negative behaviour cycles

I want to sidestep a little here, as this is such a crucial concept to understand. I'm often questioned by distraught adults desperately trying to support young people about their child seemingly revelling in the misery and upset that their behaviour causes others. You may have experienced a young person smiling or laughing when in the throes of a negative behaviour cycle and it can really push our buttons.

A person who doesn't feel good in any given moment will find their own ways to feel better, even if they are dysfunctional. Some children will seek an adult to talk to or to comfort them, others will listen to music or play sports, others may lose themselves in video games to escape the outside world momentarily. Others will escalate their behaviour to feel anything other than the uncomfortable feelings that they're experiencing, whether that be embarrassment, shame, inadequacy, fear, anxiety, injustice – the list goes on.

Now, what trips many of us up – no blame, no shame – is that when a child is in a negative thought–feeling–action cycle, the way in which others respond to them compounds the negative thoughts about themselves, and so the cycle begins again. For example, a child who thinks that they're not good enough, for one reason or another, then feels inadequate and so acts in ways that are considered to be rude. Those around them then respond to the rudeness and that compounds their feelings of fear and unworthiness, and so they act out the way they feel. The cycle goes around again, and they become stuck in the negative patterns. The child then becomes so familiar with their negative thought–feeling–action cycle that it becomes almost comforting for them, as the familiarity of upsetting everyone feels far safer than the unknown.

The good news is we can support young people to break negative cycles and practising a helicopter perspective is a great place to start in your support of them.

Understanding rather than demanding

Think back to Jamie, who would cry and shout at her parents to go away, but then follow them into the next room and continue to cry and shout. Her parents were inconsistent in their responses to her: at times they would try to appease her, hoping that it would calm things in the moment, and at other times, at their wits' end, *they* would also cry and shout.

A big breakthrough for them was simply practising the belief that all behaviour is a communication of need and an expression of emotion – so as we saw in previous chapters, this involved getting into the right mindset before taking action.

That helped them become understanding (which is different from accepting, by the way) of certain behaviours, which had a positive impact on their thought–feeling–action cycle. For Jamie's parents it felt like nothing was working and so, understandably, they kept changing their responses to Jamie in the hope that something would eventually work. Once they understood their daughter's need for emotional connection (even though initially they couldn't understand why she expressed the need in this way), they were able to become more consistent and therefore emotionally stable in their responses. In the moment they would acknowledge that they could see and hear Jamie and remained firm with this, even when she yelled at them that she didn't care. Following this, they'd then reaffirm the **boundary and expectation**: 'I can see and hear that you're not happy with us right now and that's OK, but we are not going to make another dinner tonight.'

Remember that during a 'moment' with the young person you're supporting – no matter the nature of the issue – ensure the child feels seen, heard and safe by reaffirming the boundary and expectation, so that what you want to see or achieve does not change, despite the presenting behaviour.

Preventative support

While strategies like 'seen, heard and safe' help connect to a child during a 'moment' by reducing frustration and opening up clearer communication, the most effective behaviour support is preventative rather than reactive. So this means also ensuring the child feels seen, heard and safe outside of 'moments' – in the humdrum of every day, when they're happy and relaxed, they'll naturally be more receptive. You'll likely be more relaxed too than when they're distressed, so these times are always more effective for teaching and learning.

For Jamie's parents, the weekends (when they were all less harried by schedules and generally felt more relaxed) became a good time to practise the tools I'd given them. As I mentioned earlier, mealtimes were often a big source of stress for the family, with Jamie refusing to eat what had been made, instead demanding something else. By consciously acting preventatively, I encouraged her parents to discuss dinners with Jamie the day before, offering her choices within boundaries. Using the **language of choice** they'd ask her, 'Would you like chicken and potatoes, or chicken and rice for dinner tomorrow?' The two choices provided every time were both meals they knew Jamie liked, but they also worked for the parents too (so they wouldn't offer something they didn't have the time or inclination to rustle up, as that would only end up introducing stress). Jamie then happily made her choice and felt that she had some control over what she'd eat – she'd been heard and offered safe control and it felt good. The following day, when her parents served the meal she'd chosen, Jamie refused to eat it. But it was her parents' reaction rather than her behaviour that was notable – they were stable and consistent in their response, by remaining calm and consistent in their tone and body language, instead of losing their cool or begrudgingly serving up a whole new meal as they used to, in the hope that she would calm down. Even though Jamie's behaviour in not wanting to eat the meal she'd chosen wasn't what they'd wanted to happen, they felt calmer in their response because they'd prepared for the scenario in advance.

Choose your moments

There are other valuable lessons you can teach as part of pre-ventative support when a child is feeling happy and receptive, and a key one is how to manage emotions when they're in a dif-ficult 'moment'. This is something I encouraged Jamie's parents to do with her, particularly in relation to the tricky mealtimes they'd been having. They did this by practising with Jamie what she would do if at dinner she refused to eat the option she'd chosen. Her parents were pleasantly surprised when Jamie came up with some suggestions for how they might respond in order to maintain the boundaries and expectations. They also discussed how that might make Jamie feel and how she could respond, including the words or language she could use to express herself. They prepared Jamie for them not changing their expectations or boundaries, and Jamie seemed to fully understand it.

At the next dinner 'moment', Jamie refused her food and yelled that she didn't care, that her parents didn't care about her, and she tried everything she could to make them revert to all of their old thought–feeling–action cycles. Her parents maintained their calm and consistency for the most part (having a helicopter perspective helped with this). When they slipped up on a couple of occasions, they didn't blame or shame themselves or each other; they recognised they were doing the best that they could while aiming for progression and not perfection, with no time pressures or constraints. They acknowledged and celebrated the increments of pro-gress with Jamie, choosing the moments when she was happy and receptive. As time went on, they all felt so much better and dinner times overall were much calmer and pleasant for all. They were no longer walking on eggshells and it felt life-changing.

Offer ongoing support instead of becoming distraught

It was vital that Jamie's parents maintained their emotional stability in the moments that Jamie was emotionally unstable. Remember that children learn more from what they see than from what they hear. So when Jamie's parents were telling her to calm down, yet they felt anything but calm, the mirror effect was in play and Jamie responded to the energy of unrest rather than the words to calm down.

When a child has the opportunity to be seen and heard and to feel emotionally safe via connecting with you, the risks of the behaviour escalating as it once did will be significantly reduced. But remember it takes practice and more practice. If you choose to address and practise sporadically, then it is unlikely to have an impact in any given 'moment', but if you prioritise this in the same way you would revision for an exam, then you'll begin to see results in the form of incremental progress. Practise this regardless of whether the young person in question is currently displaying low-, medium- or high-level behaviours; it will benefit every child. You'll find that you'll get out what you put in. Take your time (we've all got different starting points) and remember, no blame, no shame.

Be what you want to see

There have been a number of studies on the complex topic of communication, and, as we saw in Chapter 1, most experts agree that a very large part of communication is nonverbal and that nearly all brain activity is unconscious. Children will often observe more of what you *do* than what you *say*, and they can be hyper-vigilant to subtle changes in your energy. If you're forcing yourself to adopt a helicopter perspective and smiling, but the smile doesn't quite reach your eyes, they'll know! Or if you're trying really hard to use the right tone of voice but it's not quite genuine, they'll know! We'll talk more about what to do and how to ensure that you genuinely feel better in the next chapter.

As described earlier, often when we are faced with undesirable behaviours, we may want to try and make the behaviour stop, or 'fix' it. Controlling through fear, pacifying or any other inconsistent responses may interrupt or numb our feelings of embarrassment, frustration, overwhelm or exhaustion momentarily. However, if we're subconsciously utilising such methods of surface-level support, we mirror this inconsistency of emotions to the children in our care and don't support them at root-cause level.

We've looked at how children will often display undesirable behaviours as their own coping mechanism, getting into negative thought–feeling–action cycles in order to try to feel in control. Preventative measures of sustained support, implementing consistent routines, expectations and boundaries, by utilising the language of choice, and addressing and practising at times when the young person is happy and feeling good significantly reduces the risk of undesirable behaviours reoccurring in the same way. This type of gentle support helps to break the negative cycles that children get into attempting to be seen, heard and feel safe.

If we can embody what we want to see in the young people

in our care, this in itself may be the most empowering and influencing strategy in your toolkit. You cannot support undesirable behaviours with undesirable behaviours, fight trauma with trauma responses, help an anxious child from a place of anxiety, or encourage and promote happiness and balance while feeling unhappy and unbalanced. We are always only doing the best from where we are, which will often have some positive impact. As we move through life, we collate more information and knowledge that supports us to build upon the existing skills and knowledge that we already possess. In the same way that progress is made in increments, we're not going from failure to success, inadequate to adequate, or from bad behaviour support to good behaviour support. We are going from good to better, from seeing some progress to seeing more progress, from existing knowledge and skills to building upon existing knowledge and skills.

The Five Cs for behaviour support

Coming up, using the example of a family I worked with in the past, you'll see the strategies I've written about so far in this chapter, now in practice. I've returned again to the Five Cs from Chapter 1 (page 46) and extended them so that they support you to clear the fog. Please ensure that you're practising the Five Steps (page 66) continually to adopt the mindset needed to successfully embed the Five Cs strategies before moving on to these extended Five Cs. Take your time to master the initial ones before starting these.

Case study

Josh was described by his mother Darlene as a typical four-year-old boy. She had no major concerns about him, but she wanted to ensure that she was doing the best that she could for her son (which of course she was, as we can only ever do the best we can from where we are). Darlene told me that Josh on occasion was unwilling to cooperate, and while she mostly felt like she handled the situation well, there were times when she questioned if there were other ways of dealing with it. This lack of cooperation would crop up a few times during their daily routine and I asked Darlene to initially choose one focus for improvement (beginning with just one area was far more manageable than tackling it all at once). Darlene chose to focus on getting ready for bed, as this was when Josh seemed to have a late burst of energy and winding down for sleep was often a protracted affair. Josh would run around the bedroom jumping on and off the bed, dance while swinging his pyjamas around his head and kiss Darlene all over her face while laughing hysterically. I worked with Darlene on using these extended Five Cs to help her maintain a consistent approach when Josh was uncooperative.

Communication. The child/young person's behaviour is communicating a need for emotional connection. *Ask why continuously — what are their needs and how can I help them?*

Firstly, Darlene and I discussed how it was perfectly normal for a four-year-old to be not all that excited about going to bed. Of course, Darlene and Josh had differing perspectives about winding down for bedtime, as most adults and children do! We looked at how although she and Josh spent most of their waking hours together, bedtime triggered an increased need for emotional connection from Josh – even though he'd be sleeping for the next ten to twelve hours, it was still a really long time for a four-year-old to be separate from his mum. This thought was creating a feeling of slight angst and fear around bedtime, so his coping mechanism was acting in ways that prolonged bedtime preparations to try and avoid feeling those emotions. Josh was communicating *I need some support* and Darlene was able to look beyond the behaviour to the feeling behind it, and understand that the support needed was *emotional* support and connection in order to balance the scales.

Calm. This moment is a teaching and learning opportunity. *Remain steady and 'be' what you want to see.*

As Darlene was able to perceive Josh's behaviour as communicating *I need emotional support and connection,* she was no longer as triggered as she sometimes became before working with me. Instead she used the moment as a teaching and learning opportunity to put into practice what they had addressed and role-played in other moments when he was happy and stable. She remained steady enough to be as she wanted Josh to be – calm, relaxed and happy in her actions, body language, facial expressions and tone, and consistent in her approach – and understood Josh would learn more from *how* she was being; that felt empowering.

Curious. What feeling is my child seeking? *Acknowledge and identify the feelings for both yourself and the child.*

From the steady place of being calm, relaxed and happy, she communicated to Josh both via her state of being and through her words, 'I can see that bedtime sometimes make you feel a little worried and it is OK to feel worried, but it is bedtime now and you will need to get dressed and go to bed. I am not going to chase you when you run around your room. If you want to connect with Mummy, we can cuddle when you are in bed for two minutes before reading your story.' Initially when implementing this, when Josh still ran around his bedroom, Darlene reminded herself that he is just 'feeling-seeking' — trying to feel emotionally connected or seek a good feeling, which can often be likened to an adrenalin rush for children. Although it made her want to stop or 'fix' the behaviour, she became comfortable with feeling uncomfortable, and she sat it out. She made a mental note to address and practise talking to him about the running around at another time, in a happy moment, and followed the Five Cs consistently.

Connect. How can I meet their emotional needs? *Implement consistent routines, expectations, boundaries and the language of choice to emotionally balance.*

Prior to the implementation of these strategies, Darlene raised the new bedtime routine and practised with Josh during the day how it would go that evening. Like Jamie's parents, she chose her moments carefully at points in the day when Josh felt happy, relaxed and receptive. As Josh was only four and couldn't yet read, she used age-appropriate cues to help him remember what to expect, and printed off, laminated and put in numbered order some pictures of:

1. nightclothes
2. a toothbrush
3. a bed
4. a child and adult hugging
5. a book

Under each picture was a blank box in which Josh could draw a tick after he'd completed each task. Throughout the process of creating the visual bedtime-routine timetable, Darlene explained the purpose of the timetable to Josh so that he understood it would support him to feel more settled before bedtime. Darlene ensured that Josh felt empowered too by allowing him to be a part of the creative process using the language of choice. *Josh, on your timetable would you like number 1 to be brushing your teeth or putting your nightclothes on?* It's important to note here that when using the language of choice, you are empowering both yourself and the young person simultaneously. Either way Josh had to brush his teeth and put his nightclothes on (adult empowerment), but Josh could decide on which order to do it (child empowerment). Darlene made it clear to Josh that once he'd chosen the order in which to carry out his routine, the expectation would be that he did each thing on the timetable every single evening. When Josh (of course) tested the boundaries and still ran around his bedroom, Darlene once again reminded herself that he was just feeling-seeking and trying to feel good, so asked him again to put on his nightclothes, brush his teeth and get into bed, so that they could have their two-minute cuddle before reading a book. The boundary was a time boundary: a two-minute cuddle (Darlene opted for a sand timer – another visual cue for Josh) and just one story per night. She maintained her position of steadiness, became more and more comfortable with feeling uncomfortable, and told herself that, *It makes sense and is OK that bedtimes are a difficult time. It makes sense and is OK that he isn't going to be 'perfect'. It makes sense and is OK that I'm feeling a little tired now. It makes sense and is OK for me to take a break if I need to. I can address and practise this part at another time.*

Convey. What does my behaviour look like in this moment from the child's perspective? *Support, acknowledge and celebrate the increments of progress consistently (for you and the young person).*

Darlene initially reflected on her own behaviour from Josh's perspective after he had gone to bed, but eventually was able to reflect in the moment as she practised the Five Cs. She acknowledged and celebrated when Josh put his nightclothes on and brushed his teeth, even though he still ran around his bedroom. She then acknowledged and celebrated when Josh put his nightclothes on, brushed his teeth and got into bed, no longer running around his bedroom, even though he begged and then cried for just one more story to be read to him. Darlene then acknowledged and celebrated when Josh put his nightclothes on, brushed his teeth, got into bed, had their two-minute hug and read one story, but still cried when she said goodnight. Eventually

Josh settled down, but occasionally got out of bed after lights-out and Darlene had to go and tuck him back in.

Darlene was able to acknowledge and celebrate how far they'd come, which was a long way in relation to her own steadiness — it felt a little forced at first, but then progressed into real calm and happiness. She acknowledged how empowering it was to know that progress was moving from fear and guilt to occasional anger at times, then to frustration, then hopefulness and then happiness. This motivated Darlene to practise the Five Cs consistently; she wasn't practising for perfection, but for progression.

Perception and mindset

It's wonderful to witness the huge changes a shift in mindset can bring about when supporting a child. Building on the first chapter of this book, I hope it's clear to see how perception is key in this journey — so much of life is perceptual! As adults we're still learning, and an important aspect of providing support is getting comfortable with feeling uncomfortable when observing undesirable behaviours. It's very freeing when a change of perspective allows you to stop trying to 'fix' behaviours, and instead see opportunities to teach and learn. Once we change beliefs that no longer serve us and we perceive behaviour as communication, we can consistently implement emotional support strategies. Some of these strategies will be implemented in the thick of it, such as 'seen, heard and safe', but more and more, you'll also get used to using them preventatively by addressing them and practising with the child in feel-good moments.

They'll reduce the risk of undesirable behaviours occurring in the same way over time, leading to fewer fractious encounters and fostering in the child more emotional stability. Just be mindful that progress is incremental and will take a varying amount of time, depending on the individual.

CHAPTER 3 ROUND-UP

- Your child is using their behaviour to communicate their big feelings. Seek connection with them to identify what those feelings are.

- Be curious rather than furious.

- Be understanding rather than demanding.

- Offer support instead of becoming distraught.

- Be what you want to see.

- Establish and maintain consistent routines, boundaries and expectations, and use the language of choice.

- Long-term preventative support is more effective than reactive measures – address and practise the strategies in this chapter in good-feeling moments only, and not when the young person is upset or in an unresponsive mood.

Dealing with rudeness

A child being rude to us, or to family members, friends or class-mates, can be really triggering, especially if we were parented or taught in a way that had a zero-tolerance policy towards it. However, it's often a young person's way of expressing them-selves and/or communicating that they are feeling stressed or anxious. Remember, it's not a personal attack on you (although it can sometimes feel that way), it's them offloading *their* uncomfortable feelings onto you. Children's brains are not yet fully developed and they will go through different stages of cognitive development in terms of language learning and information processing. This means it's to be expected that they will not act as adults do. Here are some ways to support children while not letting it get to you.

The upcoming suggestions are covered in more detail throughout the book: follow the page references to learn more.

Be what you want to see (page 103): Don't ride the wave of emotions with the child – be the lifeboat in the storm. Show them in your responses what it is that you want to see from them. If you'd like to see them calm rather than stressed, then model that to them. It's what you do more than what you say that will be the biggest learning tool when dealing with rudeness. You'll be able to achieve this if you are consistently maintaining your own wellbeing and you are not emotionally full (page 119).

Emotional support (page 111): Validate a young person's feelings using the 'seen, heard and safe' technique (don't worry, in doing so, you're not validating the behaviour, just the feeling behind it) and then reaffirm the boundary and expectation (page 217).

Emotional connection (page 128): A secure attachment between yourself and the young person is key. Maintain regular and consistent connection time to reduce the risk of the rudeness reoccurring.

Prevention practice: Rehearse and practise *what to do when...* with the child. Young people often default to subconscious behaviours when feeling stressed or anxious. In good-feeling moments, when they're not emotionally full, practise other ways they might release frustration or stress without resorting to rudeness. Then acknowledge and celebrate with them the incremental progress (page 73).

4

Wellbeing: Theirs and Yours

Have we ever been so busy? Or time-poor? Juggling so much, with never ending to-do lists adding to the pressure of always being 'on' and reachable, we're never off duty. Most of us are spinning plates of family life, work, relationships, caring duties and a whole ream of other responsibilities; it can feel like squeezing in anything extra might cause all those precariously balanced plates to come crashing down. Since I'm encouraging you to adopt a whole new approach to support your child, making this a priority among the many other demands of life can be a lot, and so *you* need support while doing so. When I'm asked how I manage to avoid becoming overloaded, my answer is always the same – for the most part I maintain my wellbeing. (I say for the most part because it's never perfect, but it is always progressive.) Looking after children, whether they're your own or in a professional setting, though often wonderful, is also exhausting. If you're also dealing with extra behavioural needs, it becomes even more draining, and so looking after yourself and staying well clear of burnout is absolutely non-negotiable.

We *all* want to feel good and emotionally safe. By this I mean we want to feel predominantly happy (no one can feel happy *all* the time) and emotionally balanced, and the ways in which we seek our need for wellness will vary from person to person. As you read this book, you're likely thinking of a specific child or children – they have learned and are still learning a variety of ways to look after themselves in order to maintain the feeling of control and therefore safety. Some young people have learned that certain behaviours mean that they can 'control' their environment temporarily, as they seek emotional connection in undesirable ways. That's why it's paramount that behaviour-support strategies go beyond the surface level and promote internal support strategies that children can eventually embody as they grow. It's vital we model this to children so they can learn how to maintain their own wellbeing, regardless of what's going on around them.

You are a priority

It's all well and good to understand behaviour-support strategies, but in order for them to be effective and have lasting impact, we need to prime ourselves to be in a position to maintain a different mindset. What this book is really about is encouraging a way of being in order to effectively support behaviour (rather than yet another long to-do list). Once we're in a positive frame of mind, everything else feels much less of a struggle. Many people feel that taking care of their personal wellbeing is indulgent or even selfish – I'm here to tell you it's not. In fact, the opposite is true: you can only take care of others if your own wellbeing is intact, so you are doing everyone around you a service too when you take time for yourself. If you skip over the suggestions in this chapter, the support you give to the children in your care will be less effective.

Setting a wellbeing example

In the previous chapter, we looked at how children learn more from what they observe the adults around them doing rather than saying. Given 93 per cent of our communication is non-verbal, that's a lot of subconscious energy for them to pick up on! In practice, this means that if you pretend to be happy, it's unlikely you'll achieve long-term behaviour modification with the young people in your care. Children know when we're faking it when we say we're fine but really aren't, when we give a tenuous smile, when we say positive words but the tone or pitch of our voice doesn't quite match up. They know when it doesn't feel right, so we really need to take this element of behaviour support seriously. I would go as far as to say that this is the most important element of support, even though it's often the part that people skip over or are casual about adopting.

It's important to note here that those suffering from mental health conditions, ranging from mild to severe, acute or chronic, can still offer children effective behaviour support. It is just paramount that *you* receive support too, which will look different for each individual. By showing young people, through your lived experiences, healthy ways to cope, you are building resilience in them. It's not about being 'perfect' (that doesn't exist anyway) or never showing 'negative' emotions, it's about being genuine and allowing yourself the support you deserve.

Case study

My friend Janine had, over the years, perfected the art of 'coping' on a surface level; however, just below the surface she was riddled with anxiety. From the outside looking in, she was successfully juggling work and raising her three children really well while maintaining her marriage and relationships with friends and family. But from her perspective, it felt like she was drowning inside. The smile she gave to the world weighed heavily on her and she felt exhausted – mentally, emotionally and physically. It was like being on a never-ending treadmill, trying to reach a destination of satisfaction and wholeness that was always slightly out of reach.

Janine was convinced that her children had no idea when she wasn't coping or how she felt beneath the surface; she certainly didn't want to burden them with her stress. Though they might not have been able to put into words what they were picking up, unbeknown to Janine they could instinctively *feel* that all wasn't well. Furthermore, what they were learning was *when we feel bad we pretend that we feel good and keep it hidden from others so that on the surface it will look like we're OK.* In turn, Janine and her husband had no idea that their children had picked up on this behaviour, as they hid it so well – they would smile and laugh on the surface (just as their mum always had), despite an underlying unease.

This is a common scenario that might resonate with you, and if so, remember no blame, no shame – we are where we are, all doing the best that we can. I can certainly relate to not always quite feeling like myself, trying to keep my head above water, juggling so many priorities – it can be a strange existence and it is far more common than you might think. We adopt different coping mechanisms (in the past mine was ensuring that everything was neat and tidy) and we become so used to these coping mechanisms because they temporarily or even for a lifetime allow us to normalise living in such states.

Coming up are the wellbeing strategies I supported Janine to implement, which over time helped her reduce her anxiety and overwhelm.

Feeling emotionally full

Imagine a glass about 90 per cent full of water. Pretend for a minute that the water is your negative emotions, so you are 90 per cent full of angst, worry, stress, overwhelm, tiredness, frustration, anger or pressure (fill in the blanks with whatever is relevant to you). If you are 90 per cent full, you then only have 10 per cent capacity to think: *reason, react and respond*. When you apply this to your thoughts, feelings and actions, a 10 per cent capacity means you're going to have an on-the-ground, in-the-traffic perspective. With that 10 per cent you are more likely than not going to see and think things that just com-pound your negative feelings and so from here your action, reaction and responses to behaviour will be impacted.

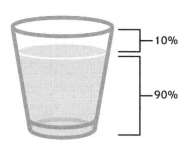

Case study

When I was a headteacher, I remember when a wonderful boy, Alfie, aged about seven, started in my school. Although Alfie often acted undesirably, I could clearly see that this was just a communication of his negative emotions about himself. So I took it upon myself every day, as I said good morning to all of the classes, to make an extra effort to say an individual good morning to him. I wanted him to feel seen, heard and safe, and every afternoon before he went home, I would say goodbye and that I looked forward to seeing him again the following day. Now on one particular day, I was very preoccupied. It was the early days of my mum's dementia diagnosis, before she'd moved in with me, when we were still getting our heads round the care she needed. At this stage in her deterioration, she'd begun wandering off out of her home, only to become disorientated and lost. I knew that if that happened, she'd be just about able to use her phone to at least answer a call and read the nearest road sign so that I could come and find her. On this particular day, I was feeling extra worried about her potentially wandering off because I had such a busy day ahead at work. I didn't know how I'd manage if she needed me too. Due to these thoughts, I spent the day feeling apprehensive, anxious and worried, and at the end of the day, when I went to Alfie as usual to say goodbye, I was surprised by his reaction. He asked me, 'Miss, what was wrong with you today? Something wasn't right.'

Alfie had no way of knowing what was going on with my mum, but he had sensed something different in my action due to my thoughts and feelings. To this day I'm not sure what it was — maybe my smile didn't quite reach my eyes or my tone of voice sounded different, or perhaps my body language was more tense than usual. What I am sure of is that because I was about 90 per cent full, I only had 10 per cent capacity to carry out my action, which altered how I acted compared to when I was less full.

Consider for a moment what fills you up. For me it's being tired, or worried about my mum's future, among other things. Become more consciously aware of your subconscious pro-grammes – that is, the subtle things that you automatically do when feeling a certain way, which you may not be consciously aware of at the time. When we do become more conscious of them, we put ourselves back in the driver's seat.

Take the wheel of life

When we prioritise our wellbeing, the quality of support we offer to children (and anyone else) is better. It's as simple as that. In order to support children to take control of the thoughts that then impact their feelings and actions, we must do the same. If you are 90 per cent full and so are the children in your care, you cannot adequately support them. We've looked at how we need to be what we want to see, and in order to genuinely 'be', we need to prioritise our own wellbeing and feelings of emotional safety. You can't jump from not feeling good to feeling great in one step, or reduce your 90 per cent fullness to 50 per cent all at once. It's not simply a switch that can be flicked. So, what's the solution? It is to protect and consistently maintain your wellbeing.

My key strategy for effective behaviour support, one that underpins my whole methodology, is this: find something (any-thing!) that makes you feel good and practise it consistently, day in, day out, even it's for just five minutes. For me, that's doing things like enjoying a cup of tea in the mornings, meditating, going for a walk, having a bath, reading a book, making a to-do list, keeping a paper diary and generally having time for myself (see pages 244 and 245 for more ideas). By consistently practising a bit of wellbeing every single day, the 90 per cent full I was feeling when my mum's health initially started deteriorating has slowly reduced. I'm now operating at something more like 30 per cent full, so have 70 per cent capacity instead of the 10 per cent that I functioned on previously. The more these little acts of self-care become ingrained in daily life, the more your glass of emotional fullness will reduce further, giving you more and more capacity to think, reason, react and respond in the way you'd like.

It is important to note here that life happens, so when something unexpected occurs in your life, it may very well fill you up again and that's OK, because if you've been actively practising your wellbeing. Instead of going from 90 per cent full to effectively spilling over, you may go from 30 per cent, for example, up to 50 per cent. Looking after your wellbeing is vital for being able to cope with events that temporarily throw you off your stride.

Use the resource on page 242 to chart how emotionally full you are.

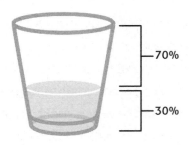

> **TRY IT:** *Make a list of what feels good to you and begin to practise it daily, literally from this moment, and then make a note of how you feel after one week, then one month and then three months (see page 245 for a resource to help).*

External support that provides internal structures

Once we've established daily care for ourselves, we are then much better placed to support the young people we're looking after. Imagine how empowering it is for a child to know that they can learn how to support themselves, that they can boost their own wellbeing when they're not feeling great. This is an amazing tool that will stay with them and can be cultivated as they mature into adulthood.

The emotional temperature check

As we've discussed in previous chapters, a child's internal feelings of emotional certainty, security and safety are nurtured when we support their psychological safety, that is, when they feel seen, heard and safe. In addition to practising routines, and gently enforcing boundaries and expectations while using the language of choice, another wellbeing tool to get in the habit of using is what I call the 'emotional temperature check'. For more information on this resource, see page 233.

In feel-good moments, when the child is happy and calm, ask them to gauge, on a thermometer scale of 1 to 10 (1 being cool and feeling calm and happy, and 10 being hot and not feeling good), where they are at that moment. Start with the cooler feelings initially, as it'll be easier for them to gauge how they're feeling when they're relaxed (cool) rather than fed up or angry (hot). Once they have identified where they think they are on the scale (this will be subjective and there's no right or wrong), validate their feelings by repeating back to them what they've expressed about how they feel. Repeat this several times in different areas of their life, for example when petting the dog, when with friends, or when listening to music. Next, move on to medium-temperature feelings and again, validate their responses and tell them that it's good to catch feelings in the moment. The act of catching the feelings in the moment will significantly reduce the risk of the feeling/temperature rising to boiling point, as well as an acknowledgement that there can be a choice to do something different. Not a choice to feel different, but a choice to act differently.

Young people, when I first meet them, often describe to me how they lose control when certain feelings surface, so the temperature check provides them with safe control. Finally, when they are used to using this tool, identify hot feelings and repeat the process. The goal is not to never feel any hot feelings ever again, but to recognise that feelings build over time and there are alternative ways to manage those feelings other than through undesirable behaviours.

The reason for doing this is so they start to become aware of how their thoughts and feelings impact on their actions. Children will often say they don't know why they react or behave as they do and are unaware that they experience a range of emotions other than feeling happy or angry. Once they become aware and in touch with their feelings, they become empowered to understand that they can steer their own ship and not be constantly swept away by the wave of their emotions. In time, the fear of certain emotions overwhelming them is reduced, as they learn to experience feelings without being carried away by them.

Every child is different, and so with a younger child you may see a behaviour – such as loud crying – repeatedly, as they're still developing other ways to communicate their needs. The thermometer won't necessarily help them to stop that behaviour in the moment (although it has been known to on occasion), but it will help them to become more emotionally literate as they grow. It will allow them to comfortably face their feelings and talk about them, instead of developing coping strategies that suppress emotions right into adulthood.

So often we try to teach in heightened moments, during a tantrum, for example, when children are too emotionally full to take in what the adult is saying. As with the glass being full, they need adequate capacity to react and respond, so remember to revisit these teaching opportunities later on, when they are calm.

Case study

Aurora was just six when I worked with her and her family on the emotional temperature check. When she was happy and not emotionally full (and so had capacity to receive guidance), her mum Rosie supported her to label her feelings as she played with her dolls. Rosie would point to the scale (a similar resource can be found on page 233) and ask Aurora how she felt in that moment. They practised this over and over again, so Aurora was able to understand how and when she felt like a 1 or 2 – like when she was playing with her dolls, or in the park with their dog Mollie, or when her uncle Andrew came over for dinner. Rosie then introduced other moments higher up on the scale, like when it was time to leave the park or when Uncle Andrew had to go home, and that felt more like 5 or 6. (Do note here that Aurora could sometimes manage the scale in these 'higher' moments, as she had practised using it in the better-feeling moments. If she was feeling overwhelmed, Rosie simply set it aside and addressed and practised it again when Aurora was feeling less emotionally full.) Eventually, Aurora was able to say for the most part when she was at an 8 or 9 on the scale, like when she was really tired and would have to put her beloved dolls away and get ready for bed. Sometimes she didn't want to and was just too full, but that was perfectly OK, as the incremental progress was evident, and they were aiming for progression and not perfection.

All of this was doable for Rosie and Aurora because Rosie continually maintained her own wellbeing in order to then successfully practise and implement the other techniques I'd introduced, such as the Five Steps (page 66) and the Five Cs (page 46). From Aurora's perspective, she felt seen, heard and safe and was learning from her mum how to 'be', how to manage emotions that manifest as behaviours without any shame or blame, time pressures or constraints. A win–win for both of them.

For older children, depending on the individual, the emotional temperature check can still be as effective; however, you may decide to add or try instead what I call the 'thought-before-feeling' technique.

The thought-before-feeling technique

Before any feeling comes a thought. As we operate from our subconscious most of the time, sometimes we're not even aware of what thoughts come *before* our feelings and instead lose ourselves in the action or reaction that comes *after* the feeling. We can support children to identify the thought in the exact same way as the emotional temperature check, starting from isolating the good feelings first. Instead of, or in addition to, pinpointing how hot or cold they are, they can also begin practising the thought that comes before the feeling. For example, before a good feeling it may be, *I really like being around that person,* or *I enjoy playing football,* or *I am good at art*; and before a negative feeling the thought may be, *I am really tired/hungry,* or *I don't like being in a big crowd,* or *I'm not good at this.* Again, the reason for this is to support children to understand how their thoughts and feelings impact on their actions and empower them to not be fearful of their emotions.

Case study

Enzo, aged fourteen, was supported by his teacher to identify things that made him feel good. He shared that he loved football, or any physical activity, as well as woodwork and playing on his PlayStation. These things all made him feel good. Enzo's teacher then helped him to ensure that he did at least one of the things that made him feel good on a daily basis and, once completed, they'd then take a temperature check and also note the thought that came before the action. Enzo was quickly able to see and (more importantly) *feel* for himself how maintaining his wellbeing impacted on his thought—feeling—action cycle. It was extremely empowering for Enzo and he felt seen, heard and in control, so in time no longer needed to seek these feelings in undesirable ways.

Once you've stabilised your own daily wellbeing routines, you can support the children in your care to do the same, then link them to the temperature check and/or the thought-before-feeling technique. As with anything, it takes practice for you and your child to become more consciously aware of your thoughts and able to react from a place of consideration rather than triggering fight-or-flight mode.

Emotional connection

Finally, one the most important wellbeing strategies for every-one, regardless of age, is emotional connection. On page 247, I include a resource to help you make emotional connection time part of your routine.

Case study

I worked with a mum, Yvonne, and daughter, Candice, on the value of emotional connection. Yvonne spent all weekend with her daughter, so she felt sure she was having plenty of emotional connection time. I could really see the positives in all this time together but supported Yvonne to perceive it slightly differently. I asked her if during this time she was totally present. At first, she said she was, but when we broke it down, Yvonne realised that she wasn't fully present, as she was sometimes cooking or cleaning, on her phone, or telling

Candice to do or not to do something. Nothing wrong in any of that. However, in order for emotional connection time to become an effective behaviour-support strategy, Yvonne needed to remain totally focused on the present moment with her daughter. This might only be for ten minutes a day if that was all she could manage. The *length* of time isn't necessarily the important part, it's the *quality* of the time spent being fully 'in the moment', preferably one on one, that's key.

Taking this into account, Yvonne and Candice decided to name this distraction-free time 'me and you time'. Her daughter thought of the name (which I'd encourage every child to do), and during that time mother and daughter rolled around on the floor laughing, just the two of them. You and your child may choose to play a game, read a book, dance to music, play a video game, go to the shops, or bake something — anything that's fun and pressure-free.

This is such a simple yet extremely powerful strategy. It is preventative, as it provides emotional connection (which is, ultimately, what we all seek), so if we can provide that for young people regularly, they won't then need to escalate their behaviour in order to feel that emotional link. Ideally, you'd start with ten minutes a day of connection time; however, if you're thinking that sounds a lot initially, depending on your situation you could break it up into two minutes at least three times a day. You could try first thing in the morning, or when your child returns home and before bed, building each two-minute slot up by two minutes over time, as and when feels comfortable and manageable. Even a hug and a kiss for a teenager before bed and telling them you love them no matter what can have a significant positive impact. We *all* need emotional connection.

Please note that it's really important that emotional connection time never be used as leverage or punishment. It should never be a case of 'If you continue to behave like this, we'll have to cancel our you and me time' (or whatever you choose to call it) or, 'Because you didn't make a good choice, we are no longer going to have our you and me time.' They must receive this time regardless because it's a crucial part of their overall wellbeing and a highly effective behaviour-support strategy (both preventative and as a remedy in tougher times). If a young person is initially refusing emotional connection time with you, don't panic! Maintain your wellbeing so that you don't take it personally and keep the space open for them should they change their mind. You can calmly remind them each day that you've set that time aside for them and that you won't fill it with anything, nor take it away. It can take a while initially for them to feel confident or comfortable with this potentially new concept or way of doing things, and that's OK. Emotional connection promotes emotional wellbeing and that leads to self-love – studies show that those who do not practise self-love are more prone to depression and anxiety and are quicker to react negatively to situations. I don't say it lightly, but prioritising my wellbeing changed my entire life, both professionally and personally. I carried from childhood many typical trauma responses, such as people-pleasing, which in turn made me self-critical, insecure and at times made me feel a lot of shame – these are all very common feelings for young people to experience. Now, I can honestly say that I hardly ever reside in such feelings for long because I carry out my wellbeing practice daily, and consistently adopt the mindset needed to give support to others by practising the Five Steps (page 66). If those feelings do rear their heads, I don't blame or shame myself, which helps me quickly turn things around and continue to progress with the support I offer. If you can understand how empowering this could be for you, then imagine the same for the young people in your care. It gives me goosebumps thinking about how transformational this is for them.

CHAPTER 4 ROUND-UP

- Protect and maintain your own wellbeing in order to effectively support young people.

- If you set an example of self-care, children will learn to prioritise their wellbeing. It's an amazing lifelong lesson to impart.

- We cannot support children effectively if we are emotionally drained ourselves.

- Use the techniques in this chapter to help children tune in to their emotions.

- We all need emotional connection. It encourages emotional wellbeing, which in turn affects our capacity for self-love.

Responding to non-compliance

A lack of cooperation from young people can drive us round the bend (particularly if we're already feeling frazzled). Non-compliance is often due to a young person exerting their want or need for control. All of the preventative strategies in this book purposely provide the child and adult with a sense of agency, significantly reducing the risk of non-compliant behaviours reoccurring.

The upcoming suggestions are covered in more detail throughout the book: follow the page references to learn more.

Routines and language: Creating daily routines *with* the child provides emotional certainty and emotional support. Incorporate any tasks they usually face with non-compliance and invite their participation, setting out their routine by using the language of choice (page 220) and providing them with safe control (page 101).

Reward and **effect:** In a good-feeling moment with a child, discuss any potential effects of them showing a lack of compliance by practising *what to do when…* Work out together how you'd navigate that and allow them to be part of the decision-making by using the language of choice (page 220).

Boundaries and **expectations** (page 217): If young people adhere to these only because of adult enforcement or fear, then the emotional safety and security that the boundaries and expectations are meant to be providing can be easily missed; instead, the child will push against them in the form of non-compliance. Support the young person to understand the boundary and to meet the expectation by explaining their purpose with a visual timetable which reflects the pre-agreed routine. Provide language support (as per the first point) and emotional support (see next point).

Emotional support: You'll never go wrong by validating a young person's feelings using 'seen, heard and safe' (page 100), and if in doubt, simply say what you see.

Emotional connection (page 128): This key element is what will support you and the child with all of the above.

part two

Guidance That Lasts

Behaviour Layers: Separating the Child From Their Behaviour

It may sound obvious, but young people need to know they are lovable and likeable, and that you enjoy their company. Feeling liked and respected – unconditionally – roots a child in safety and gives them the security to know that we can see past inevitable mistakes.

In previous chapters we've looked at how our thoughts are so powerful because they shape the perceptions that then ultimately create our reality. The reality for a child who believes they are naughty is that naughtiness becomes their identity and so they live up to who they believe they are – it can become a self-fulfilling prophecy. A child who feels they are difficult to like or love will go on to have many of the feelings we've been exploring so far and then communicate these feelings via undesirable behaviours. Whereas a child who understands that the behaviour was undesirable but knows they are still likeable and lovable can literally transform their reality and perception of themselves. Knowing they are liked and loved unconditionally can positively alter their thought, feeling and action over time. Showing a young person that we see beyond their behaviour is win-win for both adult and child because it helps maintain the wellbeing for both parties, which in turn prepares your mindset for long-term progress.

Emotional layers

Guilt and shame are two of the lowest emotions we can feel. They're also the most unproductive. It's a common belief that if children feel a little bit of guilt or shame, they may not then repeat the undesirable behaviour. This is simply not the case. In fact, what happens is that guilt and shame most often produce more guilt and shame behaviours, such as recklessness, lying and negative self-talk, keeping young people stuck in a negative thought–feeling–action cycle.

Case study

Madeline and Roman had two children, Cleo, aged nine, and Riley, who was seven. They were concerned about Riley's behaviour towards his elder brother Cleo, to whom he was sometimes physically aggressive. Riley was also extremely demanding of his parents' time and attention. He would regularly and deliberately shout over them if they were talking to each other or speaking with his brother; even if they were on the phone, Riley had to interrupt. He would dominate family situations in a bid to become the centre of attention and seemed to relish upsetting his brother by doing things like switching off his PlayStation mid-game, then laughing. His demands felt constant and his parents were drained.

In an attempt to get Riley to understand the effect his behaviour was having on not just Cleo, but the entire family, Madeline and Roman would say to Riley, 'Look at how you've made your brother feel. He loves you but doesn't want to play with you now if you're going to be horrible. We feel really sad and disappointed about this, Riley. Why do you keep doing it?' (This kind of response may ring a bell with you and if so, remember no blame, no shame. An awful lot of us have been there and of course we're just trying to do the best that we can from where we are in any given moment.)

From Riley's perspective, his parents' reaction made him think along the lines of *I am a really horrible boy. I make my brother sad and disappoint my mum and dad. I am not very nice.* These thoughts about himself would lead to feelings of guilt, shame, unworthiness and embarrassment. Thinking back to the glass analogy in the previous chapter, Riley was emotionally full, at about 97 or 98 per cent capacity, and the more guilty and shameful he felt, the fuller he became. This meant Riley only had 2 or 3 per cent from which to act and respond, so not much capacity to absorb the message his parents were trying to convey in order to modify his behaviour. The only way to reduce Riley's fullness would be to support him to feel good. Good-feeling thoughts are what help to balance the scales and reduce emotional fullness. The thought that he was horrible and a disappointment kept him stuck in a negative thought–feeling–action cycle, repeating undesirable behaviours over and over again.

We know that Riley was emotionally full but how emotionally full would you say his parents typically were in these situations? Maybe 90–95 per cent? So Madeline and Roman would only have had 5 per cent capacity to think, reason, react and respond to Riley. With this in mind, my first port of call didn't start with Riley but with his parents and their need to prioritise their self-care.

Remember the power of perception

By consistently practising wellbeing, Madeline and Roman significantly reduced how emotionally full they were, which created more capacity to act, react and respond. They could more easily adopt a helicopter perspective, from which they could separate Riley from his behaviour *and* perceive the behaviour as a communication. This can be done as simply as thinking, as this will positively alter your perception, or saying to a child in a similar situation to Riley, *I don't like it when you hurt your brother. It's the behaviour I don't like, but we really like you. You do so many kind and thoughtful things.* What this does is support the child to absorb what's being communicated to them about their behaviour without them becoming too emotionally full. This is because, if they can still hold some belief that they are a wonderful human being who has just made a wrong choice, the guilt and shame doesn't take hold in the same way. It allows them to believe that they have the capacity to do better, even if they make mistakes more than once, as it's not *who* they are, but a choice they made. It provides them with an element of control, which helps them to feel safe.

It's important to note here that if a child, even a very young child, has had years of believing themselves to be 'naughty' or any other similar term, it's unlikely that they'll believe what you say when they first hear you separating them from their behaviour. It's paramount that if they don't respond in the way you'd like, or if they even verbalise disbelief, you shouldn't respond to this secondary behaviour and try to convince them otherwise if you're met with a wall of disbelief. If that is how the child feels at that time, validate their feelings, but just be mindful not to go down the path of disbelief with them (avoid going down a rabbit hole of 'Yes, I am naughty,' 'No, you're not,' and so on). Breaking habits can be uncomfortable, but facing our feelings head on, knowing that it is OK to feel them, is how we come out the other side.

Our mindset can help break *their* negative cycles

Think about a habit that you've broken or are trying to break. It could be smoking, snacking, biting your nails or scrolling through your phone. Now think about how hard it is to stop, even though the reasons that you want to are really positive. It's not easy because the behaviours you want to change have become part of a thought–feeling–action cycle, and the habit or the action is actually providing some comfort to you at this point. It is meeting a need, even though you want it to stop. It could be that **thoughts** around going to a work meeting or dropping your child off at school lead to **feelings** of nervousness for one reason or another, and the **action** or the behaviour is to bite your nails as a way of releasing the nervous energy. What conscious or subconscious behaviours do you have that you would like to change or stop, that have become habitual? I'm always fascinated when I notice on public transport how many of us (me included) find it difficult to 'do nothing' or to be present, and how for some of us (no blame or shame), our phone provides a comfort that gives us something to do, as a way of distracting us and releasing that restless energy. In a similar way, children habitually repeat undesirable behaviours, even though they may cause them stress, as the familiarity may be comforting.

When young people experience uncomfortable feelings, they release that energy in a number of ways, whether that's shouting, crying or stomping off, and those behaviours can become habitual: *When I **feel** X, I **do** Y.* What can make it difficult to break the negative cycle is the reactions of those around the child – how their behaviour makes *us* feel can then impact directly on *our* thought, feeling and action, not only about the behaviour, but about the child themselves. If we think, *They are so obnoxious and rude*, we need to make a subtle yet powerful shift that allows us to separate the child from their behaviour, which will allow us to alter our perception, giving us the space to perceive the behaviour as communication. If we can shift our perception to, *Their behaviour is so obnoxious and rude,* this acknowledgement doesn't fill us up as much – to, say, 80 per cent, leaving 20 per cent capacity to think, reason, react and respond. From here it's easier to follow the thought, *Their behaviour is so obnoxious and rude,* with, *What are they trying to communicate via their behaviour? What are they trying to tell me?* Whereas, from the initial thought, *They are so obnoxious and rude,* it is far more difficult to follow on with, *What are they trying to communicate?* as that first thought often originates from, or leads to thoughts that fill us up such as, *They are doing this on purpose to annoy me* or, *They know exactly what they're doing but do it anyway.*

This is a reminder of why behaviour support must begin as a mindset rather than jumping in headfirst with list of strategies, which won't stick.

> **TRY IT:** *Focus on a particular behaviour that you would like to support a child with. Make a note of how the behaviour honestly makes you feel and how emotionally full you think you are when confronted with it. Then, after thirty days, repeat the exercise. You may notice that the behaviour makes you feel the same, but you are less emotionally full when confronted with it, so can begin to separate the child from their behaviour. Or you may notice that you feel different and are less emotionally full. Either way, your perception will begin to alter after these thirty days of consistent, conscious wellbeing practices.*

Separating a child from their behaviour works best when you truly believe it, so before you verbalise it to them, I would suggest doing this exercise first. Remember 93 per cent of our communication is nonverbal, so it's likely that the child will pick up on you not being entirely genuine if that is where you currently are (which is absolutely fine, if so). This book is written in a way that you work on mastering one area before moving on to the next, although the different areas can overlap, depending on your starting point (which will be different for every individual). Allow yourself time to digest and practise so that eventually these practices will become a way of being for you, rather than yet another point on your to-do list.

No regression, only progression

If at any point implementing any of these practices feels like a struggle, take a moment to look at the beginning of the wellbeing chart below – this will always help to reset and rebalance. Normalise the fact that you will most likely go back to the beginning numerous times over the upcoming months and years. We are human beings doing the best that we can and it's perfectly normal to forget, become inconsistent at times, want things to move quicker or want to give up! Remember, perfection doesn't exist and self-awareness *is* progression. The more we practise the tools to make this our default mindset, the more it becomes embedded, making this type of positive behaviour support second nature (and incredibly effective).

Wellbeing prepares the mindset.

Continuously practise the Five Steps (page 66)
to maintain the mindset.

From this mindset implement the Five Cs (page 46).

As you implement the Five Cs, acknowledge and
celebrate the incremental progress.

CHAPTER 5 ROUND-UP

- Guilt and shame often produce *more* guilt and shame-based behaviours.

- Separating the child from their behaviour supports them to absorb what is being communicated to them about their behaviour without the child becoming too emotionally full.

- Breaking habits can be uncomfortable, but by facing them head-on, we come out the other side.

- The subtle yet powerful shift of separating the child from their behaviour alters our perception and allows us space to perceive the behaviour as communication.

- Our thoughts are powerful and shape our perceptions, ultimately creating our reality.

Gentle Guidance

Motivating young people

Often what we see as important or a priority is perceived rather differently by a child. A good way to motivate young people is to try to understand from their perspective – think back to when you were younger: did the thought of washing up excite you? No? Me neither! Instead of trying to get a child to be excited about a clean and tidy house (as we may be), support them to understand the whys behind our requests and be OK with the fact that they may never like washing up!

The upcoming suggestions are covered in more detail throughout the book: follow the page references to learn more.

The bigger picture: For younger children, visual aids, such as a timetable, help them to see the bigger picture and know that the thing that they are unmotivated by is just a part of life and not their entire life. It is often the feeling associated with the thing that can overwhelm young people: for example, the thought of having to go to school when they'd rather be home with their dog, snuggled up in front of the TV, can feel torturous! They need to see the steps involved in their day unfolding: for example, after school they'll come home, take off their uniform, undertake some homework or household tasks and then cosy up with the dog. A visual timetable helps them see when they can get to do the things that they enjoy, as well as those they're less keen on (but are a necessity of life).

For older children, you can support them to understand how their goals and desires marry up with the present moment and the skills or action steps – step-by-step things that they can do – they need to reach their goals. For example, if a young person wants to be a professional football player, you might explain to them how valuable it is to be able to work as a team, and how that skill can be developed by collaborating with family and classmates. Similarly, the discipline required of a footballer is a skill that might begin at home, where there are responsibilities to take care of. You can talk about handling disappointments, overcoming setbacks, and so on in a similar way.

Routines and **language:** Creating daily routines with the child provides emotional certainty and emotional support. Incorporate any tasks that they are often unmotivated by (but need to do) into their routine, working together with them to set out expectations. Using the language of choice (page 220) will provide them with safe control (page 101).

Boundaries and **expectations** (page 217): Often when young people begin to feel a sense of accomplishment, pride or independence in reaching an expectation, they also begin to feel more motivated. Support them to understand the boundary and to meet the expectation – some find a visual timetable that reflects the pre-agreed routine helpful in boosting motivation.

Emotional support: Validate a young person's feelings via 'seen, heard and safe' and strengthen emotional connection (page 128). Remember it's OK for them to feel as they do.

6

Interpret Behaviour, Validate Feelings

When my godson Ravi, who has a diagnosis of autism, was younger, his speech was less developed than his peers. Classmates and neighbourhood children, who often couldn't understand him, would ask his sister what he was trying to say. She would interpret for him until he learned different ways to successfully communicate with his friends. Ravi's frustration at not being able to communicate with words in the same way as his peers often led him to throw something or tense his body and scream, and his sister would calmly soothe him. It was fascinating to observe her instinctively validating his feelings, and even at a tender age she understood that when he lashed out, although it was distressing, it was never personal. One day when they were out playing and Ravi pushed another little boy, Jason, over, I overheard her say to him, 'It's OK – I know you're angry, but Jason didn't know that you wanted his ball. You can't have it now because we're playing with it, but you can play with another one and when we've finished the match, we'll play a game with you.' She was interpreting his behaviour by understanding that pushing Jason was his way of communicating his desire to play with the ball. She was also validating his feelings by acknowledging that he was angry, in essence applying 'seen, heard and safe' (though that was unknown to her).

Part of our role in supporting young people is to decipher what it is that they are communicating to us via their behaviour. In this chapter we'll be looking at why validating feelings is a central principle of effective support and how it interlinks with the topics covered in the preceding chapters. Validation can impact positively on our thought–feeling–action cycle, and in order for it to be authentic and impactful, the foundation of wellbeing should already be laid, so that the young person can *feel* that the validation is meaningful and not just some spiel being regurgitated. This authenticity is the subtle but powerful difference between behaviour support that doesn't 'work' or only lasts for a while, and behaviour support and modification that is sustainable over time. When we're able to offer support from an emotionally balanced perspective, the way in which we receive and interpret behaviour, the way we support and validate feelings, and how it then positively affects behaviour over time becomes more impactful.

Remember that the bulk of behaviour-support work should not be done in the heat of the moment but when the child (and adult) is feeling better, and that's because it's hard to think past how we feel. This may take a while to get your head round initially, particularly if you've previously sought out or tested methods to stop a behaviour the minute it occurs. Trying to 'fix' behaviour in a moment is like battling a raging fire, constantly trying to stay on top of it as it spreads, and becoming exhausted in the process.

Perception and wellbeing underpin emotional validation

You can't think beyond how you feel. Think of a time when you weren't feeling too great and a well-meaning friend, colleague or family member gave you some advice. Unsolicited advice, I might add! You wished they'd said nothing at all – logically you knew what they were saying made sense, but due to how you were feeling at the time, logic wasn't what you wanted or needed. I've been on either side of this, both as the well-meaning friend and as the recipient of the advice. As the giver, you offer advice based on how you feel in that moment, but as the recipient, how you receive that advice also depends on how you feel.

When I perceive my two teenage children to be doing well and I'm feeling proud, happy and confident, and my cousin Dee tells me about the frustrations of raising her teenage son, my advice may be along the lines of, 'Don't worry, he'll grow out of that, Dee, it's not as bad as it seems in this moment,' or, 'Try to look at the bigger picture.' So as the advice-giver I'm able to think positively, as I'm feeling positive. As the receiver, if Dee in that moment is full of angst, annoyance and frustration, her response may be, 'That's easy for you to say, you don't under-stand,' or even, 'That's not helpful right now.' As the receiver of the advice, it's difficult for Dee to think positively when she feels opposed and is emotionally full. We know by this stage in the book that our perspectives are massively influenced by the emotional capacity we are operating on.

It's only when Dee consistently maintains her wellbeing – even when it naturally fluctuates, say between 40 and 60 per cent, depending on what's going on in her life – that she'll have the capacity to think more clearly than if she was 90 per cent full. And exactly the same applies for children. If they are emotionally full, it is extremely difficult for them to think past how they feel in that moment. It's only by validating their feelings that you'll forge connection, and this in turn will aid in breaking a negative thought–feeling–action cycle. This will allow us to be able to recognise that a snappy or defensive response is due to a child being emotionally full. It doesn't mean that we accept or condone such behaviours, but that we understand them for what they are (changing our perspective on them in this way means they won't interfere with our own wellbeing).

Becoming an interpreter

The upcoming case study shows the importance of us tuning into a child's emotions in order to interpret (where possible) the whys behind behaviours. This will help us to uncover what the young person is trying to communicate and decide on the best plan to support them adequately and effectively.

By way of background to the following story, trauma is the emotional response to an event (rather than the event itself), and how we process a traumatic event is different for everyone. For example, two children can both have a pet die: one child may be sad, cry and feel down for a while, whereas another child may feel completely devastated, resulting in a more intense emotional imprint left on the brain. Trauma can cause your brain to remain in a state of hypervigilance and effectively trap you in a state of very strong emotional reactivity; it's why, when people recall something traumatic from the past, it's often accompanied by a physical response such as feeling faint, shaking or being sick. This is the reason perception is so important to understand when supporting behaviour – what one person may perceive as a not particularly significant event may be extremely traumatic from another's perspective. We are all uniquely different, regardless of circumstances, even if we've been brought up in the same household. With this in mind, you often hear parents describe their children as reacting very differently from each other to a similar experience or teachers saying with surprise how different their classes are from one year to the next.

Case study

Mikaela was seven when I started working with her. She was described by school staff as a 'drama queen', stubborn and disrespectful in her lack of responses to them, often 'shutting down' when being spoken to. Her teacher told me that even when sent to the headteacher, who spoke to her in a stern tone, she would refuse to answer her. I was told that when her teachers raised their voices, even if this was not directed to her, she became deeply unsettled. Unbeknown to them, what was happening was that the raised voices were immediately transporting Mikaela back to hearing her mum shouting at her stepdad. Even though Mikaela didn't recall what those arguments were about and her mum and stepdad had since separated, the shouting left a strong emotional imprint. For years after, if she heard even a slightly raised voice, her body reacted as if it had time-travelled back to the past. It would lead her behaviour to change, and she would go into herself, not responding to anyone or anything. This was misinterpreted by the adults around her, who labelled her as rude, defiant and deliberately not listening to authority figures, but the reality was far from this. Hearing loud voices was so triggering for her that she'd go into survival mode, unable to think beyond how she felt in those distressing moments.

The body is like an unconscious mind, and it is very hard to create a future or move forward day to day when your body feels stuck in the past. It can literally feel like it did in a past situation, even if it's years after the event. The adults in Mikaela's life were trying to help her by saying things in the moment such as, 'Mikaela, think about what you can do differently next time,' or 'Consider how that makes your mum feel when…' or 'Try to understand that we just want to help you' (no blame, no shame). Mikaela simply couldn't think beyond how she felt in those moments and so they went round and round in circles – her shutting down led her teachers to become frustrated, which made them question her when she simply couldn't respond. It impacted negatively on her thought–feeling–action, keeping them all stuck in a negative cycle.

The good news is that we can recondition the body, meaning that when we think and feel something that is uncomfortable, we can choose a different action instead. It takes time, practice and patience and, alongside this, it's paramount to maintain wellbeing and acknowledge incremental progress. If we are maintaining our wellbeing, our emotional cup isn't as full and we have more capacity to think, reason, react and respond. We're then in the strongest position to become an interpreter of behaviour by becoming consciously aware of what thoughts lead to which feelings, and then intentionally choosing a more desirable behaviour instead of resorting to unconscious, undesirable ones.

> **TRY IT:** *Think of a negative experience, only going as far as is comfortable for you. Sit in the memory of that experience for a short while and notice how your body feels. You might literally feel as you did then, even though the event itself is now in the past.*

There are no 'wrong' feelings

A key aspect of my support philosophy is that there are no 'wrong' feelings to have. While you may not wish to accept certain behaviour, it's important to accept the feelings behind it. Becoming curious rather than furious (see page 97 for a refresher) will help you to see past a child's behavioural response. By modelling curiosity, you'll encourage them to also become curious about how they respond to certain emotions. For example, if a child becomes agitated doing schoolwork or homework and is then verbally aggressive and storms off, instead of potentially reprimanding them, interpret their behaviour as a communication, starting by validating their feelings. They could be reacting that way to the work, thinking, *I can't do this* or, *I'm not good at writing/reading* or, *This is going to be hard,* which leads to feelings of anxiety, fear, shame or embarrassment – it's these feelings that result in the undesirable behaviour. Allow them to feel their emotions and support them to know that it is 100 per cent OK to *feel* as they do, by verbally validating them, then maintain the boundary and expectation while ensuring they feel seen, heard and safe. For example: 'I can see that you're feeling anxious about this work. Let's take a one-minute break and then we'll look at it again together.'

Avoid labelling emotions as 'good' or 'bad', so that when a child feels negative emotions (and they will because we *all* do), they don't feel guilty about it. Help them to allow their body to feel the emotion and settle down into the present moment. This can be done simply by labelling the emotion and sitting with them in a way that feels safe and supportive. For example, 'I can see that you're feeling anxious and that's OK, I'm here to support you.' Then depending on the child and circumstances, either give them a hug, put a hand on their shoulder, remain in close proximity to them or sit with them in silence for a moment. This will help them to realise over time that their emotions do not have power over them and that we do not need to be afraid of them, as they help us to understand what's going on for us (for example, the underlying emotions in the schoolwork example were a fear of not being able to achieve). Once the need is revealed, it can then be supported and met, so emotions are helpful not harmful.

Many scientists conclude that 95 per cent of us, by the time we become mature adults, operate from a set of memorised behaviours in the subconscious mind. Therefore, if we can support children and young people to act, react and respond more consciously, so they learn about what thoughts and feeling lead to certain behaviours, they can in time become more conscious when thoughts provoke uncomfortable feelings (which would normally lead to them reacting in unconscious, repetitive ways).

Validation in practice

I find the most straightforward way to validate a young person's (or anyone's) feelings in the heat of a 'moment' is to simply say what I see. For example, 'I can see that you're feeling frustrated,' or, 'I can hear that you're really upset,' or, 'I understand why you feel that way and it's OK to feel like that.' This is a really important initial step in connecting with a child when they're upset. Whatever the situation, via their behaviour they're usually trying to communicate: *I feel [angry/sad/fed up, for example]… NOTICE ME!*

Validating feelings does not mean condoning behaviour or letting them 'get away' with something. It means that you're recognising and understanding the whys *behind* the behaviour and the feelings that are communicated *via* the behaviour, no matter how undesirable it is. It enables you to support from the root by not trying to treat the symptoms without understanding the underlying cause. Try not to get distracted or respond negatively to any secondary behaviour at this point, for example if they escalate their behaviour or respond to you along the lines of, 'You don't understand,' or 'You've no idea how I'm feeling.' In these potential moments, fall back to showing them they're seen, heard and safe by verbally validating their feelings and maintaining the boundary and expectation.

There are no magic words or ways to end a tantrum or outburst (more's the pity!). During a 'moment', maintain your calm, stay connected and accept all of their *feelings*. I realise I'm making it all sound so easy, when I know from experience it's not. But with practice, it *does* get easier. Once the 'moment' has passed and the child is calm and happy again, gently revisit it as a teaching opportunity.

Validating feelings helps a child tune in to their emotions

Young people need to know that their feelings *can* change and what once made them feel anxious and angry, like homework, doesn't need to remain that way for ever. Once we become an interpreter and identify the thoughts and feelings that come before the action, we also change our perception, as we can then know what the need is and how we can help support the child to meet that need. If you are using the emotional temperature-check strategy (page 233), begin to integrate validating *all* of their emotions, whether they're positive or negative. When a child is feeling really good, identify and label that emotion, so that via you identifying, labelling and accepting all of their emotions — not the behaviour, but the *emotions* behind the behaviour — in time, so will they. Once they have more insight as they grow (even from a very young age — in fact the younger you can support and guide them, the better), they will normalise becoming curious about their feelings. Emotions then gradually begin to lose the 'scary' element attached to them that makes us want to run away from them or express them in undesirable ways when we don't know what else to do with them.

When we can accept all feelings and emotions as indicators of where we are, this is a true embodiment of no blame, no shame. This perspective will encourage them away from the ways society has more typically handled big feelings, whether that's suppressing emotions, having outbursts, pretending to feel differently from the way we really we do or blaming and shaming others for how we feel. I'm hopeful that new generations, more connected to their emotions, will replace the more rigid ways of dealing with feelings many of us grew up with.

Remember to take care of you

Remember to validate your own emotions too! Be mindful that if you are triggered by a child's behaviours, it is also a gentle reminder for you to pay attention to you. Their behaviour is triggering something in you and once we can interpret this as such, it helps us see where we need to grow. Gently guiding young people gets easier when you regulate your own emotions and stay connected with your child.

CHAPTER 6 ROUND-UP

- You cannot think beyond how you feel.

- Look at the whys behind the behaviour. Remember that behaviour is a way of communication.

- We can recondition the body, but it takes time, practice and patience.

- Embrace all emotions and try not to label them as 'good' or 'bad'.

- Emotions are signs of an unmet need, so they're helpful rather than harmful.

- Validating feelings helps you connect with a child, making them feel seen, heard and safe.

- Looking after your wellbeing helps you to validate the feelings of others.

Gentle Guidance

Reconnecting and repairing after a fracture

It is perfectly OK to not be OK. When young people can see that we experience a range of feelings too, we become more relatable to them. There is sometimes a danger (no blame or shame) in keeping our children away from seeing how we feel, as they may then think that we don't understand when they feel similar emotions. Similarly, they may also think that it's not OK to feel certain feelings and so try to hide or bury them the way that they perceive us to be doing, only then to find undesirable coping strategies (page 56) as a means of channelling those emotions. All emotions have to 'come out' in one way or another; if not, our bodies can hold on to them and cause physical ailments such as headaches, body pain or illness, so showing young people that it's OK not to be OK sometimes, and how to deal with that in healthier ways, means that they are more likely to listen and respond when we want to repair after a fracture.

The upcoming suggestions are covered in more detail throughout the book: follow the page references to learn more.

Own it: If you've lost your temper (no blame or shame, you're only human and we've all been there), own it. Apologise to your child and explain the thoughts and feelings behind the action, for example, 'I'm sorry that I shouted at you – I was feeling tired.' Be careful not to assert blame or shame elsewhere, such as, 'I'm sorry that I shouted at you, but because you weren't listening, it made me mad.' We are all responsible for our own actions and feelings, and we always have a choice in how we respond to a scenario (I find this really empowering).

Gentle guidance helps *everyone*: Routines, boundaries, expectations and conscious use of language provide emotional certainty, safety, security and support for your child *and* for you too! When you're consistent in these areas, it can be used as an emotional safety net in more challenging times and supports you to be stable, reducing the likelihood of fractures reoccurring in the same way.

Wellbeing (page 115) and **emotional connection** (page 128): Maintaining your wellbeing is paramount because it gives you more capacity to support a child, and emotional connection is key for strengthening your bond. Both can help you to perceive the young person and their behaviour differently, reducing the stress and anxiety for both adult and child that often leads to fractures.

Pre-Pave the Way: The Behaviour Journey

The tools in this book all aim to gear you up for a preventative approach to supporting children, because that's always the most effective way. I'm not a proponent of gimmicks or quick fixes: they're not long-term solutions. Imagine you're going on a long road trip. Prior to setting off it's likely that you'll check your car tyres, fill the tank with fuel and ensure you have plenty of water and snacks for the trip. This is pre-paving: you're being preventative rather than reactive by preparing for any potential bumps in the road. Though you haven't eliminated the possibility of bumps cropping up, you've prepared for them in the best way that you can.

Though all children are uniquely different, there is a common denominator, which my gentle approach is based on: the primal want and need to feel emotionally safe. If we can pre-pave the way as a child grows and develops, we can help them make sense of their emotions and provide them with the security they need to flourish as their true selves. As ever, our role as we facilitate pre-paving the way begins with us being in the right frame of mind, and this can be hard to absorb because we tend to be natural doers – we want to prematurely leap into action with tricks and hacks. However, the 'doing' is hardly ever sustained if the mindset is not laid down as the foundation. I recently heard a sports commentator say of a famous tennis player, 'Her mindset was off today, so she didn't perform as well as expected.' It made me realise that despite the tennis player having trained for months, if not years, working closely with her trainer on strategy and positioning on the court in order to win matches, on the day, if she didn't have the right mindset, it would be game over.

Pre-paving the way is supported through the topics covered in the chapters so far, most notably by creating positive, sustainable habits, taking care of our mindset and offering consistency in our care of the young people in our lives. We'll look at these more closely in this chapter, alongside some practical support we can offer children, as well as preventative rather than reactive tips that you can try straight away.

Old habits die hard

Have you ever tried to give something up or create new positive habits, where you begin with gusto, but before long, lose your stride and find yourself back to where you were originally? It's completely normal that most of us find it difficult to change our behaviour. I can't tell you how many times I've tried to eat healthier or get fitter, only for my good intentions to fall by the wayside after a week or two. One of the reasons we find ourselves stuck in cycles of behaviour is because they are so familiar, and it's far easier to revert to familiar habits than to create new ones, even when we believe they'll be better for us in the long term.

When it comes to children, we might often say or think, *Why do they keep doing that when they know I won't be happy about it?* Or, *If they don't want to hear me nagging, why do that again!* Or one that I find myself replaying to my children, *How many times do I need to tell you the same thing?!* Just as we find it hard to break the habits of a lifetime or create new ones, so too do our children. Even if they know it may be better long term to do or not do something, it takes time, repetition and consistency to form new habits. Children's brains are not yet fully developed and while as adults we may be more likely to respond more rationally to situations from our prefrontal cortex, children are more likely to respond emotionally from their amygdala. So when we think or say, *You know better – what were you thinking?* the reality is no, they were not thinking in the same way that we do, as their brains are not as developed as ours. I find this fact fascinating and empowering – reminding ourselves of this physiological difference in a 'moment' with a child can help us perceive their behaviour differently, which in turn has a positive impact on how we gently guide and support children with their behaviour.

Mindset

As I've said (once or twice already!), adjusting your mindset is your primary tool for pre-paving the way for effective behavioural support. I'm not saying we need to have a positive mindset every single day of our lives (and some would find that more difficult than others), but what *is* important is conscious awareness. If we are consciously aware of our thought–feeling–action cycle, it immediately places us in a better position when supporting children. It is OK to not feel on top of your game and to experience negative emotions, but it is not OK to project our negative behaviours onto others. If we can teach children this through the behaviour we model, it can be one of the most empowering lessons for them to learn as they grow.

Case study

Amber, single mum to Penelope, aged two, came to me as she was battling with anxiety and depression, and she was concerned it was affecting her parenting. She told me that some days she struggled to get out of bed, but Penelope kept her going. (Before beginning any work, I checked with her that she had sought and was receiving support for her mental health needs, and she was.) She was doing the absolute best that she could from where she was (as we all are). Amber told me that she was extremely preoccupied by other people's opinions of her and how she parented. She wished that she didn't care what others thought of her, but would become very affected by what she perceived others were thinking of her and her daughter, particularly during heated moments, like when Penelope had a tantrum.

The first thing we worked on together was Amber's mindset, beginning with perception. Just by challenging her perception of tantrums, she felt a bit better — she began to tell herself over and over again, *Tantrums are not 'poor' behaviour — they are an expression of an emotion that has become too much for Penelope.* Perceiving Penelope's behaviour in this way made her feel empowered because the behaviour made more sense to her, and although she still became flustered and even embarrassed at times, it felt a bit more tolerable.

If we perceive that parenting or supporting children should fit into some sort of ideal, then we will always be disappointed or feel like we're failing or 'not doing it right'. There is no ideal situation or method – sorry! We all have different tolerances and triggers, and so we'll all support the children in our care differently. How we raise/teach/support our children is one of the most emotive topics out there, which everyone seems to have an opinion on. At some point you'll likely encounter someone who, with a negative comment or two, tries to undermine your instincts by telling you how they'd do it differently, so prime and protect your mindset as much as you can with your daily well-being strategies (see Chapter 4).

It's the journey, not the destination

This is *such* an important concept. If you have an end goal with regard to a child's behaviour, meaning you delay all gratification, it's likely that you'll live in a state of constant dissatisfaction. Every single child continues to grow and develop in their own unique ways *for ever,* so let's embrace the journey and become curious along the way, acknowledging and celebrating the incremental progress. Remember to avoid seeking perfection and focus instead on progression, enjoying the ride without fixating on an end point. This will make the behaviour journey as your child grows a much more pleasant experience for all.

Progress swings back and forth

As explored at the beginning of this chapter, it's difficult to release old behaviour patterns. Our brains are designed to take shortcuts and go back to what they know best. What often happens, no blame or shame, when a child swings back to old patterns of behaviour, is that we think, *It's not working* or *We've gone back to square one.* Whereas if, in those swing-back moments, we maintain consistency and perceive it as *This is expected as they grow and learn – their brains aren't fully developed yet* and *Children are naturally more impulsive,* it gives us the emotional strength to keep going. So, remember that swinging back to old, comfortable, albeit undesirable behaviour patterns is behaviour progress! Acknowledging and celebrating the incremental progress at these points will help you to move through these times. Look back at the examples of incremental progress for toddler Joanna (page 77) and teenager Liam (page 79) for reassurance if you need it.

One thought at a time

You don't go from dissatisfied to satisfied in one fell swoop. Before reaching a feeling of satisfaction, you might actually experience many emotions in between that are all progress steps. But this can be completely overlooked as progress if the emotions are perceived as negative. Have you ever considered that feeling angry is actually better than feeling fearful? Take a look at these emotional stepping stones, which show that moving from one stepping stone to the next is all progress on the journey (for more on this, see the resources in Chapter 10).

Looking at our emotions from this perspective, you can see that fear is just one step away from anger, but it's still a step in the right direction. Similarly, feelings of overwhelm are better than residing in feelings of guilt.

Please note that with this stepping stones analogy, I'm talking about the *feeling* rather than behaviour, as you might think, as you read this, of the *actions* associated with the feelings, so you may immediately think of shouting when you read *angry* or shaking when you read *fear*. This is all absolutely fine, and children do the same thing, subconsciously associating a feeling with a behaviour – it's why we often see the repeat of behaviours when a child is angry, for example. However, what I'm highlighting here is that we can have a feeling and choose a different action, but that is more likely to be possible if we are able to perceive the feelings as OK to have and feel in the first place. In practice this might mean that you can feel really angry but not shout at someone, or feel frustrated and not be rude to anyone. They are not bad feelings, but indicators of where we are or of an emotional need that may need to be addressed. If we feel or a child feels guilt or shame for feeling a certain way, it becomes far more difficult to potentially change the action or the behaviour that's attached to the feeling. While it's OK to feel any feeling, it's not OK to project that feeling onto another in the form of a harmful action, for example, through verbal or physical aggression when feeling angry.

Remind yourself and teach the children in your care that it is OK to *feel* as you do. Utilise these stepping stones for yourself and your children as an extra tool to support the acknowledgement and celebration of incremental progress. You are doing great, and remember that progress swings, so if you or your child find yourself in a place of fear, it's OK, maintain your wellbeing, take your time and move through the points below to swing forward once again. Let's normalise the idea that this is what progression looks like, and look again at the illustration in Chapter 5 (page 144) as a reminder.

Preventative rather than reactive

Remember the car analogy from the start of this chapter – prevention is better than cure, and where possible we should focus our energy into preventative rather than reactive measures. If you have read and begun to implement any of the tools from this book already, then you have begun pre-paving the way. They offer a long-term approach and mentality and to complement that, there are also plenty of other preventative tools that you can get in the habit of incorporating into your daily routine with children, which can start benefiting them today and make life a little smoother.

Coming up are some examples of how we can support preventatively rather than reactively. The first common scenario is for a younger child and the second one is for an older child, but you'll notice the suggested ways to respond are very similar.

Case study

I receive a lot of queries from parents and teachers working with young children about how to respond during a tantrum. I like to reassure them there are ways to try and prevent them happening in the first place. Children love to know what to expect, even for something as common as a trip to the playground or a request to tidy away their toys. Knowing what to expect provides your child with the emotional certainty of what will happen, which reduces anxiety and soothes stress. So, before any 'event', big or small, set out a mini itinerary, talking them through each stage of the plan so they are clear on how it will play out. It's always best to start with/practise the seemingly smaller things like a trip to the park, as both adult and child can feel empowered by the success of it, rather than aiming for something bigger initially, which may work less well, leaving everyone feeling dejected.

Depending on the child, their age, their needs and the scenario, you can role-play the situation, use a visual timetable or simply discuss it with them in advance on more than one occasion. Use the language of choice in the preparation stage to provide them with safe control — offer two choices (both agreeable to you), for example, *When it's time to leave the park, do you want to have one more turn on the slide or five more pushes on the swings?* Or, *When it's time to leave Nanny's house, do you want Mummy to help you put your shoes on or Nanny?* Then, when it is time to leave, present them with the *same* pre-practised choices. Maintain the expectation and the boundaries by sticking to what you pre-agreed/practised and remember, if it doesn't go smoothly the first time, that's OK; practise again at a later stage when the child is feeling better. Be sure to acknowledge any incremental progress. For example, they may initially choose the option to have one more go on the slide and then have a meltdown, but that *is* progress! Simply them knowing that there is another option and them being able to choose from the pre-planned choices, despite their disappointed feelings, is progress, as before they may have just automatically reverted to old behaviour patterns and lain on the ground, screaming.

To ensure preventative strategies become effective with children of all ages, you need to maintain consistency and emotional connection, and as ever, protect your own wellbeing.

Case study

For older children, routines, language, expectations and boundaries are as important and impactful as with younger ones.

Let's say you're having trouble with the time your child gets home after going out with friends.

In a moment when they (and you) are feeling good, set out a mini plan for their particular situation (a visual timetable can sometimes be useful, despite them being older). This provides your child with the emotional certainty of what will happen, reducing anxiety and soothing stress – remember that stress may manifest more obviously in a younger child, but all ages experience such feelings. Ask them for their thoughts on the topic (so in this example, they might have thoughts around what time they'd like to come home) and actively listen to their responses. Use the language of choice in the preparation stage to provide them with safe control – by allowing them to be an active part of this process, you validate their feelings, helping them to feel seen, heard and safe. For example, 'I do understand that you'd like to stay out until midnight. I would have wanted to also at your age. When you're a bit older we can revisit that. For now can you think of a time before 9 p.m.?' You can also add other choices depending on your situation, such as, 'Would you like to message me when you're on your way home, or should I message you – which do you prefer?' Talk them through each stage of the routine before they go out so they are clear about how it will play out, including if they were to return home late. For example, 'If you're more than five minutes late home, do you think you should have to be home half an hour earlier next time, or should you miss the next evening out but come home at 9 p.m. the time after that?'

Then, maintain the expectation and the boundaries by sticking to what you pre-agreed, and remember, if it doesn't go smoothly the first time that's OK. Speak with them again when they are feeling good and acknowledge the incremental progress. Focus on what has gone well, for example if they got home late but messaged on their way. Rather than potentially reprimanding them for being late, say, 'Thank you for messaging me on your way home – that is really responsible of you,' and then maintain the boundary of what you'd previously agreed about being late. That part has already been pre-discussed, so if you're consistent, it allows you the freedom of maintaining expectations and boundaries while still leaving room for praise and recognition of the incremental progress. This is ultimately what will spur them on to continue to 'do better', as the better someone feels, the better they will act, react or behave.

Routines	=	emotional certainty
Language	=	emotional support
Expectations	=	emotional security
Boundaries	=	emotional safety

CHAPTER 7 ROUND-UP

- It is far easier to revert to familiar habits of behaviour than to create new ones.

- It takes time, repetition and consistency to form new habits, but it can be done.

- Adults are more likely to respond rationally to situations, whereas children are more likely to respond emotionally.

- Behaviour progress swings – it can feel like two steps forward, one step back, but you *are* making progress.

- Be preventative rather than reactive where possible.

Rewards

We're all motivated in life by feelings. We want things for the feeling that we believe we'll get once we have them, so just be mindful of this when considering rewards for young people. If the reward makes them feel proud, independent, happy, accomplished or recognised, then that is the motivation. Feeling good is the best type of reward for any individual, and when a young person feels good, they behave more desirably. I'm often asked which rewards are best, but it really is different for different children, and here are a few things to keep in mind:

- Reward the effort rather than outcome; rewards should never be used to bribe a young person, but to support their growth and progress.

- Verbal rewards are often the best type as, ultimately, it's about feeling good. Although there is absolutely nothing wrong with tangible rewards, a reward alone will never be enough to motivate a young person; it is the emotional connection or the feeling behind the reward that makes it impactful. So if a young person is rewarded by someone they have a secure attachment with, that will feel much better than if it's someone they're not as close to.

The upcoming suggestions are covered in more detail throughout the book: follow the page references to learn more.

Incremental progress (page 73): Acknowledging and celebrating progress, however small, is one of the best ways to motivate young people (as well as ourselves). So often we focus on getting children to battle through something they don't want to do by dangling a carrot – for example 'If you finish your homework, you can watch a movie.' The length of time before starting homework and completing it can feel interminable to a child (especially if they're counting down the minutes until they can watch that film), which is why they may feel disgruntled before the work has even begun. What I've found much more effective is to support young people as they progress through a task. For example, when they sit down to do their homework, acknowledge and celebrate that they've done so, maybe despite feeling like they don't want to (you can validate feelings via 'seen, heard and safe', see page 100). Then after five minutes, acknowledge and celebrate what they've done so far (and continue to repeat at intervals), which will help them to feel supported and empowered to complete their task step by step.

Avoid projecting your feelings: It's common to hear parents or teachers use phrases like, 'It makes me really sad when you behave in that way,' or, 'It makes me really happy when you behave in this way' (no blame or shame). Children are not responsible for our happiness and when their thoughts and feelings are burdened with that responsibility, their action is often to behave in undesirable ways. It doesn't feel good to know that 'it's my fault that you're unhappy' and this can result in a child becoming stuck in a negative thought–feeling–action cycle (page 53). Instead, rephrase feedback along these lines: 'I'm so proud of you and you should be really proud of yourself,' or, 'That really shows how responsible or independent you are.'

Say it before you see it: When we offer positive feedback before a young person has even demonstrated the praise-worthy behaviour, it communicates to them that you trust and believe in them. Affirm to young people, 'This is going to be a successful lesson today,' at the start of class and then support them step by step to achieve that goal via incremental progress (as in the first point above). Remember that success doesn't necessarily mean that a trip to the park is going to be smooth sailing from start to finish. Success can be a child crying when it was time to leave but without lying on the ground, or a teenager who returns home late but by ten minutes instead of an hour like the previous time. Acknowledge and celebrate all these small steps in the right direction; it keeps both adult and child motivated so that they can continue to progress. Be precise with the praise so that children know how to recreate that good-feeling moment. Often when we speak in generalities like 'well done' or 'good job', it can be hard for a child to know which part of whatever it is they've done has warranted your encouragement, so home in on something specific in their efforts to celebrate.

Emotional connection (page 128): The attachment you have with a young person (which can be strengthened through emotional connection time) can impact on how they respond to a reward. Receiving a reward of any kind, be it tangible or verbal recognition such as praise, will feel so much more meaningful for them if it is from a person they have an attachment with.

Water What You Want to Grow

When you plant a seed, you water it, provide sunlight and continue to nurture it until it blooms. When you first begin to water it, it looks like nothing is happening, but you continue to care for it daily without frustration or any uncomfortable feelings. This is because you're confident and unquestioning that something is happening beneath the soil, and as long as you consistently nurture it, it will grow. You can easily adopt this mindset because when you water the seed, despite no sign of growth on the surface, it doesn't trigger you in any way – it doesn't make you feel unworthy or like you're failing the seed, or that others are judging you because it hasn't yet bloomed. You are calmly and gently determined to maintain consistent watering until it's ready. You are calmly and gently focused on what it will become and expecting that something positive will occur. For our children, if we water only what we want to grow and focus with calm and gentle determination on their positive aspects, sooner or later that's what we'll predominantly see. Positive aspects will become the dominant perception when we think of the behaviour of the children in our care or talk about them, and because we have shifted our focus, what they mirror back to us will be mostly positive.

In this chapter we will be delving deeper into how powerful focus is when supporting behaviour and how what we think about creates our reality. Children will live up to what is expected of them and what they are known for with regard to their behaviour. By watering what we want to grow in young people, we help them to separate themselves from their behaviour so that they understand that *who* they are is not a problem or causing upset, rather it's their behaviour that is undesirable. When we create this separation by watering what we want to grow, they will understand that they are wanted and accepted, and feel empowered to modify their behaviour with our gentle guidance and support. I've included some exercises later in the chapter, which will help you initiate and/ or build on emotional connection, which is the all-important factor for growth.

Focus on what you'd like to see

Think about a time when you were in your car rushing to get somewhere. Suddenly every traffic light seems to be red and you think to yourself, *Typical, when I'm in a hurry, all I experience are delays! What an annoying coincidence*, or *How unfortunate*. The thing is, it's not a coincidence, it's perspective and conscious awareness. What you think about, be it consciously, subconsciously or unconsciously, appears in your reality, as what you look for, you will always see. When you're having a bad day and everything *seems* to be going wrong, that's because from that perspective everything 'wrong' stands out, whereas on a day when things are going well, what may have annoyed you previously doesn't affect you in quite the same way. The same applies to children and their behaviour – when we anticipate that their behaviour is going to be unbearable on a day out, for example, throughout that day all their 'unbearable' behaviour will stand out and you will most likely think to yourself, *I knew it, the day has turned out to be just as predicted!* However, if you've been nurturing your mindset, the way you perceive that behaviour and how you think, feel and react to it will be vastly different – behaviours that would previously have been experienced as unbearable will be perceived differently for both you and your child. Just as in the flower example at the start, when you purposely focus on what it is that you want to see from young people and water what you want to grow, that is what will stand out to you and for them. Have faith that their behaviour will meet expectations in increments over time.

In practice, as ever, this begins with you. For example, if you're asking them to do something or if they have a task to carry out, tell them with confidence that you trust them to complete it and thank them before they've even met the expectation. Keep the task small, manageable and achievable, and acknowledge the incremental progress (remember, there's no such thing as perfection), so you might say something along these lines:

'I trust that you are always doing the best you can.'

'I've noticed that you've been making an effort.'

'Thank you for picking your clothes up from the floor.'

'Thank you for coming into class and sitting down right away.'

You'll be amazed to see the results of this strategy if your words are delivered from an emotionally balanced place and you have been maintaining your emotional connection. This often sets a positive tone that continues, but if it doesn't, it's important, should they do something undesirable in the next moment, not to follow up with something like, 'You were doing so well and now you've ruined it,' or, 'I was so pleased with you; now I'm disappointed.' Progress is incremental, and regardless of what potentially happens next, they are doing well and nothing is ruined. In fact, that increment of progress should be acknowledged and celebrated with no buts (this will be more achievable if you're maintaining your own wellbeing).

Case study

I recently asked my nineteen-year-old son to repaint the bathroom walls (this level of DIY isn't an everyday task in our household, but I do think it's important for all members of the family to pitch in). I gave him some notice, asking him in advance, rather than just springing it on him. I used the language of choice with him beforehand: 'Would you like to do the painting on Wednesday or on Saturday?' which provided him with safe control (but ultimately two choices I was happy with). He chose Saturday (the day furthest away!) but when Saturday came round, he asked me, 'Do I have to do to this now? Can I do it tomorrow?' I practise my wellbeing daily (some days are better than others), but generally because of this I operate at around 30 per cent full. This means that when my son grumpily asked me if he could paint on another day, I was able to adopt a helicopter perspective with my 70 per cent capacity to react and respond and consider: *It's perfectly understandable that a nineteen-year-old would rather go out with his friends on a Saturday then paint the bathroom! I'd have felt exactly the same at his age. This is not him being disrespectful to me.* In my response I wanted to ensure he felt seen, heard and safe, so I validated his feelings and reasserted the boundaries and expectations: 'I can hear from your tone that you'd rather not paint today. I do understand that you would rather be out with your friends. You made the choice to paint today instead of Wednesday, so if you get started now, you can still meet your friends afterwards. Would you like to start now and see your friends afterwards, or paint later and see your friends on a different day? Thank you for doing this.'

I'm sure you can guess which my son chose! A win-win for all. He painted the bathroom, but still felt that he had some control. Had I been more emotionally full, it's far more likely that I would have perceived his behaviour differently and my response would also have been different. I know this as I have past experience of it! I would most likely have thought, *I gave him a choice but he's still asking for another option! Why can't he do this one thing for me? This whole approach just isn't working.* Making him feel seen, heard and safe wouldn't even have entered my thought process, and instead for the rest of the day all I'd think and feel, and therefore see and respond to, would be a continuation of my frustration.

You'll note I thanked my son before he had even begun and didn't get drawn in or distracted by his grumpy tone. I remained focused on watering what I wanted to grow, which was his helpful and kind characteristics. Being a grumpy teenager doesn't mean that he is not a wonderful person; it means that he felt grumpy in that moment and not that he is a grumpy person. Imagine if your colleagues could see you when you were having a disagreement with your partner or on a day when you were feeling tired and fed up and so labelled you as a rude or arrogant person. You would think to yourself, *That's not who I am as a person; I am a nice person – I just behaved in a certain way that was undesirable.* It is so easy to fall into the trope of characterising our children as 'stubborn', 'naughty' or something similar, but when we do, they live up to it because they think it's what we expect from them. Then when we observe 'stubborn' or 'naughty' behaviour, we feel justified in having labelled them and so that thought–feeling–action cycle remains active. No blame or shame – for years I used to joke and say that my son was lazy and he would forget his head if it wasn't attached to his body! But as I learned about the power of words, I changed my language, which altered my perception completely – and what I began to see in my son changed too. Use the power of words to water what you want to grow and support the young people in your care to foster and nurture those qualities you'd like to see instead.

Making our conscious efforts subconscious

As we've looked at in previous chapters, we operate most of the time from our subconscious, the part of our mind that can make decisions without us needing to consciously or actively think about them. Because of the role of the subconscious, you'll likely need to actively override your default settings when trying to implement any new behaviour-support strategies initially. It might feel like you're falling back on the old cliché of 'fake it till you make it', as you attempt to smile through gritted teeth during a toddler or teenage tantrum because of how it subconsciously makes you feel, for one reason or another. On the surface we may understand why a child might be behaving as they are, but in the heat of the moment the theory can go out the window and we lose our cool. How we react to the behaviour in front of us can then leave us feeling disappointed or deflated.

In Chapter 3 we looked at how it's not possible to support undesirable behaviours with undesirable behaviours, or promote happiness and balance while feeling unhappy and unbalanced ourselves (no blame, no shame). This is why I'm such an advocate of first ensuring our mindset is set up to be a foundation for long-term, lifelong positive behaviour support. The 'fake it till you make it' approach won't be effective, as young people pick up more on our feelings and the energy we give than what we say – and they can tell from an extremely young age when that appears to be contradictory.

So how do we embed our conscious habits into our subconscious? By giving it practice and time, and by watering what you want to grow. All the guidance in this book is interconnected rather than standalone – in order to effectively water what you want to grow, you must simultaneously be maintaining your wellbeing and the emotional connection with the children in your care. It takes both to adopt a new mindset, and because behaviour progress swings back and forth, your frame of mind from the outset is paramount to maintaining focus and hope that things will continue to progress (remember that acknowledging incremental progress helps immensely with this).

It's OK to lose your cool – it doesn't mean you're a horrible parent or a bad teacher or that you're not doing it 'right'. You are a human being doing the best that you can from where you are – more than that, you're taking time to add to the knowledge you already possess to support you on the road of continuous progression. We need to practise maintaining our mindset because of how powerful the subconscious mind is, despite our on-the-surface determination to support children or to do something differently. By watering what you want to grow, this focuses the mind to purposely think something different from before. This is why I was able to ignore my son's grumpiness when he was asked to paint the bathroom, rather than resort back to previous negative subconscious thought patterns that would have most likely produced more undesirable behaviour. I mindfully practised focusing in on the positive even before it occurred.

The work will pay off because, just like practising reframing our perceptions, eventually conscious practice *will* become subconscious practice, making your responses when supporting young people become second nature.

> **TRY THIS:** *While you're in the shower, try to stay completely focused on how the water feels against your skin. Sounds simple, right? What you'll find, however, is that it's extremely difficult to do, as your mind will keep wandering off 'all by itself' to things embedded within your subconscious mind. The subconscious (both adult's and child's) is so powerful, which is why it takes time and practice to change the thought–feeling–action cycle. It is doable, though, and extremely empowering and effective with practice.*

Practise giving uplifting feedback

As with the seed analogy at the start of this chapter, the children in our care require consistent nurture, even when we can't see anything happening in terms of immediate changes in their behaviour. Something *is* always happening beneath the surface, and it is gradual. A seed doesn't form a fully bloomed flower overnight, but we don't have to wait until it has become a flower to feel a sense of pride and achievement. We gently and consistently acknowledge and celebrate every shoot, each increment of progress along the way, and because of that, the flower goes from strength to strength. If we cease to nurture the flower, it's obvious that it will most likely wilt and its growth will be impacted. I'd like you to take a minute to consider how often you communicate joy and happiness *directly* to the children in your care. If you've already begun implementing wellbeing strategies, you may find this easier to think about than if you've not yet begun to implement them (and remember, no blame or shame).

Case study

My friend Danielle recently told me that her teenage son Dean had said to her that she's always nagging and moaning at him. Danielle was upset and annoyed that he had the cheek to say this to her when, as she told me, 'I do everything for him. He's so fortunate and he just said that to me to be obnoxious.'

In my response I was conscious that it's difficult to think beyond how you feel, and in that moment Danielle was feeling upset and annoyed, so I validated her feelings (which as we know is different from agreeing with them). I waited until she was feeling calmer and happier (just like I'd do with young people) before I spoke with her about perspective. I know how much Danielle loves her son and I know that Dean knows that too. However, from Dean's perspective, in the past couple of years he felt that the main feedback he was getting from his mum was frustration and annoyance (at his teenage antics!). When I spoke with Danielle about this, she immediately responded, 'I do tell him positive things all the time!' However, after contemplating it further, with no blame or shame, she realised that the 'all the time' was actually just a few times in as many months. When she really thought about the majority of their conversations, they were along the lines of, 'Dean you haven't done what I've asked you to do yet again...' Taking a step back, it occurred to her that her son had a point.

For the record, there's nothing wrong at all in talking to young people about what they should or shouldn't be doing; just consider the emotional scale (page 32) and ensure that the emotional connection is equal to or outweighs this, as what you focus on will always dominate. This is why I speak so strongly about perception, as you'll *always* see what you're looking for and this is why children will often say or think things like, *You're always picking on me*, or *I'm always getting told off.* In turn, our response, whether we think or say it is, *That's because you're always doing things that warrant you being spoken to!* And so the cycle continues. To break the cycle our mindset needs to change so that we can perceive differently. The undesirable behaviour may still occur, but the way you understand it alters the way you perceive it, and so how you feel about it, and then how you react and respond to it. We can't take away the behaviour in the moment, but by continuous nurturing, we can deactivate it over time and be mindful of reactivation.

Practise connection

Caring for children can feel all-consuming, and in the hustle and bustle of everyday life, it can be easy to forget the importance of connection with our children. For parents, connection can be established in lots of ways, like showing affection, allowing them to see that you love spending time with them, and letting your child know you've been thinking of them if you've been apart. Depending on where you are in prioritising your wellbeing – so whether you're at the very beginning, focusing more on self-care, or if it's well established – you can try some or all of the following strategies to enhance your practices and water what you want to grow. I'm hoping this book will be one that you come back to time and time again. The first time you read it, you may try just the first of the upcoming exercises, however the next time you may feel ready to try more. Take your time and do only what feels right for you.

This first exercise is for anyone, even if you haven't yet started actively practising my wellbeing strategies (page 115).

Leave your child a picture or a note, depending on their age, saying something like, 'I love you and hope you have a great day.' End the note with 'see you later at home', or something similar, to reinforce emotional connection. This is a simple and effective way of communicating **directly** to them how valued and loved they are. If you're a teacher, you could leave them a Post-it note at school or a comment in their book expressing that you are proud of their efforts and that you look forward to their contribution or continued efforts in their upcoming lessons.

When you do see them later in the day, instead of asking them, 'How was school today?' or 'What did you do today?', try, 'I'm really happy to see you' or 'I'm happy that you're home.'

This is another simple and effective way of communicating emotional connection **directly** to them.

For years, I used to get frustrated when I didn't receive from my children the desired response from a simple question like 'How was your day today?' I'd often receive a grunt or monosyllabic answer, at best! Like many other parents, this would irritate me, and would often lead me to trying to assert control through fear, demanding an answer or verbalising to them that their lacklustre response made me feel sad (no blame, no shame). What I eventually realised was that, instead, I needed to provide safe control and emotional connection. I now know that even if I don't receive an enthusiastic response in these situations, they have received my emotional connection. So, rest assured that however they react, you are nurturing them without the pressure to have a specific response, and something is happening beneath the surface, just like the watered seed.

Recommended if you've been practising your wellbeing/nurturing your mindset for a while.

Here's another exercise to try, with variations depending on whether you're a parent or offering support in a school/organisational setting. These should only be tried if you've been maintaining your wellbeing by continually practising the Five Steps (page 66), implementing the Five Cs (page 46) and acknowledging and celebrating incremental progress. This is because children will know when the words feel scripted or forced, and a foundation of a balanced mindset is the most solid upon which to build these strategies. Initially it may feel a bit unnatural, but that's OK and to be expected; just maintain consistency – as the street artist, Banksy, once said, 'Learn to rest, not to quit.' Try these tips in calmer moments, when the young person is generally feeling good and receptive to connection.

- Before leaving the house, as they're putting their coat on, name the things you love about them.

- When they sit down at their classroom desk, acknowledge that you've noticed their presence, or throughout the lesson acknowledge their effort in a short, clear sentence, including a point of emotional connection, 'I can see that you've really made an effort to get started. I'll be back again to check in on how you're doing.'

Find opportunities to tell children (appropriate to your role and relationship with them):

- Your opinions matter to me and you are safe to disagree with me.
- Your feelings are important.
- I think you're amazing.
- I love you.

Celebrate the positives

What was the last conversation you had about your child/ their behaviour and who was it with? It's really typical to find ourselves stuck in a cycle of complaining about our children (among other gripes!) and this can sometimes be to our detriment. In future discussions about your child, start a new momentum by finding something positive to say about them or talk about something else entirely. It's so easy to fall back into subconscious ways of being, where we have a moan about our child or their behaviour, but by focusing on some positive aspects, this will eventually take precedence in our consciousness. This may be harder to do initially, but that's OK, keep practising!

As we've explored, the words we choose to speak are extremely powerful in impacting upon our experiences and perspectives. When we say positive things to ourselves and to others, it begins to imprint on our subconscious mind, as described earlier. Find something positive to say about your child, however small, that you believe (if you can't initially think of something, focus on something they're good at). How young people hear us talking to one another, as well as to them, tells them about you and them, and our thought–feeling–action impacts on theirs. This isn't about lying to yourself or others, and of course it's OK to confide in others about undesirable behaviours (having the opportunity to offload is essential!), just find an increment of progress to add to every discussion too.

If you are struggling in any way to find a positive, then find something else that is positive to focus on and be appropriately honest with the children in your care. If you're not feeling great and you have projected that onto them or to someone else, then apologise unreservedly by taking ownership rather than blaming others. This is just as powerful as maintaining positivity as far as we're able to, because it demonstrates to children that they are worthy of love and respect, and it normalises progression over perfection.

Try this only if you've been continuously practising your wellbeing/mindset and can easily acknowledge incremental progress.

For one week, treat your child as if they were already behaving as desired. This is the most impactful if you can match that energy yourself with what it is you want to see from them. If you want them to not raise their voice when frustrated, for example, are you doing the same? Once this strategy is mastered, you will find yourself responding as if the child has shown desirable behaviour (even if they haven't) in any given moment. This strategy is preventative and if you practise, it will reduce the risk of undesirable behaviours reoccurring in the same way. Address any presenting behaviours in the moment with 'seen, heard and safe' (page 100) and remember you are looking for incremental steps of progress (which you'll see) rather than an overnight transformation.

Just like the painting example with my son, when he complained initially about doing it, I responded from a place of expecting him to do the job and do it well. This then impacted positively on his behaviour as he mirrored my calm response, then got on with the job and learned some valuable lessons about behaviour in the process, while still feeling good about himself.

When watering what you want to grow and focusing on positive aspects, a child, just like a plant, will only grow to the size of the pot it is in while in your care, so what you expect to see is what you will see from them.

CHAPTER 8 ROUND-UP

- What you think about, be it consciously, subconsciously or unconsciously, appears in your reality.

- Young people will pick up more on how we feel than what we say.

- It takes time and practice to adopt a new mindset because behaviour progress swings.

- Children still require consistent nurture, even when we can't see anything happening in terms of immediate changes in their behaviour.

- What you focus on will always dominate.

- The words we choose to speak are extremely powerful, impacting upon our experiences and perspectives.

Gentle Guidance

Advocating for young people

Years ago, when one of my mum's foster sons started secondary school, she was called into the school for a meeting. My foster brother had a diagnosed need and so the special educational needs coordinator at the time led the meeting and started by saying that they had grave concerns regarding his behaviour. My mum was told that he was using his height (he was tall for his age) to intimidate teachers and that they were unsure as to whether he would be able to succeed at their school. As a result, he was at risk of exclusion. My mum, a slight woman in stature, sitting at their large table attended by several senior staff members, responded, 'I'm a small woman and a single foster carer, yet I'm not intimidated by him. If I can adequately support this young boy alone, then you can support him collectively. He's not going to be excluded and *he* doesn't have to change to fit into your school; *you* need to adapt to meet his needs.'

In retrospect, this was an amazing early lesson in behavioural support. From this point onwards, I began to become consciously aware of what it was that my mum was specifically *doing* that was so successful for the young people she cared for. My foster brother was not excluded and did go on to succeed at secondary school. This was entirely down to those key adults around him.

There may be times when you feel that the child you're supporting is misunderstood or that others aren't adequately meeting their needs. You may even have spoken up, only to feel like no one is listening, making you feel alone and sometimes with the added stress of feeling like the situation is getting worse instead of better. You are not alone. There are so many wonderful practitioners, services and support groups out there to liaise with, once we know where to look (if you're in the UK, your GP or local borough website are good places to start, and there are some useful organisations listed on page 253).

Children often have a variety of needs that can't be met by one individual or a single organisation's support. Gentle guidance will support *all* young people; however, if a child has sensory needs, attention deficit hyperactivity disorder (ADHD), autism or another diagnosed need, they will require additional, multiagency support from specialist services that meet a multitude of needs for any young person.

Identify need: The referral process for assessments can be frustratingly long and it can be tempting to think, *Well, what's the point waiting a year or longer to see a specialist?* But hang in there, it's worth the wait.

See the bigger picture, as it can make a difference for the rest of a young person's life. If you're not sure whether extra support is needed, just ask – it's always better to eliminate a potential need than not have it identified at all. If you're unsure who to seek advice from in the first instance, speak to your child's school or, if they're not in school, go to your GP and they can signpost you. It can be daunting to begin finding the right support for your child but, if you can, start as early in their schooling as possible. Further down the road, it's worth appealing a decision if you disagree with what the authorities have decided is appropriate to meet your child's needs while they are at school.

Support groups: Peer groups or other forms of group support can be empowering and inspiring for you and your child, especially to share common experiences with others who may be going through something similar. Having an outlet to voice frustrations can be really cathartic; be sure to extend those discussions to what you can do now in order to keep finding a way forward.

Agree a plan: When discussing the best ways forward, any adults involved in supporting the child should identify the common goal(s) and generate discussions from there. As a collective, aim to agree what steps need to be taken to achieve the goals, as well as any extra support required to facilitate the process. If you've had similar discussions in the past that haven't gone well or failed to bring about the resolutions you wanted, try to reframe the new approach, entering into it with a positive mindset. It can be easy to keep focusing on what hasn't worked in the past (no blame or shame) especially if things were traumatic for you or your child, or left you feeling let down, but try to separate past experiences from what's happening now. If you are working on rectifying something that's happened previously, try to do that separately from any new discussions so that in the latter, you can focus on injecting positive energy into moving forward.

part three

Behaviour Strategies

There is No 'End' to Behaviour Support

For years I suffered with tension headaches, and shoulder and neck pain. As a busy mum, I couldn't handle all of these ailments interfering with everyday life, so for several years I took prescription medication that mostly dulled the pain and allowed me to get on with things. For many people, medication for similar conditions is an absolute lifeline that improves their quality of life immeasurably. For me, though, it got to the point that the side effects of the medication were outweighing the benefits, and so I re-evaluated my situation based on my wants and needs. I wanted the pain to go, but I no longer wanted that to be via medication. I wanted to stop waiting for the next headache or neck and shoulder pain to arrive before treating it and instead reduce the risk of them recurring in the first place. It occurred to me that the only way I could achieve long-term relief was to properly invest in my wellbeing by dedicating time to myself; maybe there was a mind-body connection to the pain I hadn't fully understood.

I went to therapy (one of the best things I've ever done) and started practising daily wellbeing strategies (page 115), which I still maintain. I got to the root causes, to the whys behind my pain, and began to heal from the inside out, so to speak. Not only do I no longer suffer neck, shoulder and head pain in the same way, but also there have been so many other unexpected benefits. My perception and therefore my thought, feeling and action cycles have been positively impacted upon. My parenting, work and relationships all improved; pretty much my entire life has been transformed.

And through gentle guidance, this is what you can achieve, too, for the children in your care. When we look beyond the behaviour, at the reasons *for* the behaviour, we can support effectively from there. Not only will you see improvements in a child's behaviour and wellbeing, but it'll have a positive impact on your own too.

I know the word 'journey' is overused when it comes to quests for self-improvement, but I'm throwing it out here too (sorry) because it really is an apt way to describe behaviour support. There are ups and downs, setbacks and leaps; there'll be times you want to scream into a pillow (do it – it can be a good release!) and other times you'll be jumping for joy at the progress you and the child in your care have made.

There will likely be times when you feel like the strategies in this book aren't working, and if that happens, check in with yourself to nurture your mindset and remember it all begins there. Rest assured, you're not going back to square one because progress veers back and forth, and just as we continue to learn and develop throughout our lifetime, behaviour support has no 'end'.

In this chapter we'll explore how powerful and freeing it is to simply change your mind, even if you've done something a certain way for years, make different choices or alter the way in which you view the bigger picture. It's inevitable that young people will face new adversities – it's part of growing up – but these adversities, when the child is adequately supported to navigate them, shape them into the most amazing human beings. Let's equip children to deal with them by working together with them to support them rather than us working *for* or *against* them.

Moving forward

Once we reach a particular stage or milestone with a child, we don't just sit back and think *OK, bye, good luck!* – instead we continue on to the next phase, supporting them in another area as they grow and develop in the best way that they can. And this is wonderful, but we have a tendency to avoid living in the moment, often delaying satisfaction or hingeing it on a milestone that hasn't yet happened. *I'll feel better when they're sleeping through the night*; then, *I'll feel better when they settle into nursery*; then, *I'll feel better when they make some friends*; then, *I'll feel better when they get their exam results/get that job/meet a partner* – the list goes on and on! It is of course natural and expected to have concern for the children in our care, as we want the best for them; however, it's also extremely important to stop and bask in each milestone. For this reason, acknowledging incremental progress (page 236) is such a powerful strategy, with the added bonus that it becomes far easier and more likely that the next milestone will be reached. Added to that, it will be a smoother journey, as you won't be carrying with you so much anxiety and stress. Whether you're a parent, carer, teacher, support worker or play another vital part, take a moment now to contemplate the positive role you play in a child's life – they're fortunate to have you!

Reframe your focus for the future

What we place our attention on and how we highlight it to the child will take precedence in their mind. If we continuously voice our worries and concerns to a young person, it can affect how they move forward. For example, a child who is constantly reminded that if they don't do well at school in English or maths, they will find it difficult to succeed later in life. They may develop strong feelings around the subject, the pressure of which could affect their performance. Focusing on one area in this way is so powerful, so why not flip – instead, highlight all the positive aspects associated with English or maths, buy fun games that support the learning in that subject and speak positively about it. This will make a significant, lasting difference to both you and them, and is a far more beneficial (and less tiresome) way of approaching it.

It's still going to be necessary to focus on areas of development, but just ensure that that focus is balanced with or outweighed by the areas you want to nurture within the child, and take time to bask before tackling the next milestone. It's so easy to 'forget' how far a child has come when there's so much further for them to go, but there'll always be more: more to do, more to learn, more to develop.

Case study

I initially started working with Fabio and his seven-year-old son Toby because Fabio wanted guidance on how he could support Toby, who was constantly getting into trouble at school. Toby's teachers had explained to Fabio that Toby was disruptive in the classroom and in the playground. The teachers also described Toby as lacking contrition after an incident – he didn't seem to take any responsibility, and instead blamed the other children for making him act with verbal or sometimes physical aggression towards them. Over time though, things began to improve as the school staff began to balance the scales for Toby via daily emotional connection time with a key adult at school, validating his feelings and consistently maintaining expectations and boundaries. Fabio reported that Toby's behaviour had become significantly more positive at school and he was far more accountable for his actions. Fabio was pleased by this, but got back in touch with me to tell me about a new problem, as Toby was beginning to answer him back at home.

As he began to explain some scenarios to me, I observed that this 'new' behaviour was making Fabio feel very stressed. The first thing we did was revisit perspective – was it understandable that a now eight-year-old might begin to answer back? Yes! It's absolutely typical for children to challenge or disagree with the adults in their lives or not want to do something we ask, and Fabio acknowledged this. So, was the 'problem' more a question of the way it made Fabio feel? Was Toby's answering back evoking uncomfortable feelings? Unpicking it all with Fabio, this was the crux of it – a change of perspective allowed him to see what was really going on and that this was another step in Toby's behaviour journey, another milestone, so Fabio had a choice. Either way, he knew he and Toby had to move forward – they could take the next steps with angst, worry and stress, or Fabio could bask in how far they'd come and highlight that to Toby, so the positives were not 'forgotten' or minimised in comparison to the areas that still needed to be developed. He wouldn't be ignoring the backchat, just ensuring that the spotlight shone brighter on the behaviours he wanted to see. Once Fabio changed his thought–feeling–action cycle, he immediately began to relax. He was apologetic, as he felt he'd jumped the gun, but I reminded him no blame, no shame, as in that moment of realisation and remembrance of our previous mindset work, the behaviour support had already begun.

Of course, he'd have another area to support his child in and there'd be more to come — just like there would for Toby at school, who'd be building his knowledge term after term, with new exams to study for, new challenges to deal with and new accomplishments to make. Even though there was always the goal to move forward, I reminded them to also reflect from time to time on how far he and Toby had come. Acknowledging and celebrating the incremental progress felt good for both of them, and from a better-feeling place, Fabio could adopt a helicopter perspective in order to continue to support and guide his son. Toby did not stop answering back straight away after this revelation, but Fabio began perceiving it differently and so his thought–feeling–action cycle positively impacted upon Toby. In time, the way in which Toby expressed himself became more desirable, as Fabio understood that Toby's answering back was communicating a need to be seen and heard, to share his perspective on things and feel that what he had to say was valid and respected. Fabio re-evaluated and reintroduced their connection time, which for them was walking the dog daily, as that was something that they both enjoyed. I encouraged Fabio to refocus on his own wellbeing, which had dissipated a little, and in time progress swung forward once again.

CHAPTER 9 ROUND-UP

The most effective behaviour support becomes a way of being over time, rather than a rigid list of 'rules' that you're desperately trying to remember to incorporate into daily life and that don't always feel achievable. Supporting children can be stressful at times, but we also want to experience joyous moments with them as regularly as possible. Below is some gentle guidance based upon the additional strategies in this chapter to ease you into your new way of life, and you may find it useful to look again at Chapter 2 in particular for greater detail.

- Integrate routines rather than rules into your lifestyle.

- Incorporate daily emotional connection and wellbeing into your routines.

- Acknowledge and celebrate incremental progress on a regular basis – and for ever!

- Each day is a fresh start – make **no blame, no shame** your mantra.

- And finally, as Henry Ford, founder of the Ford Motor Company, said, 'Don't find fault, find a remedy.' For long-term success, try to understand the whys behind the behaviour and be preventative rather than reactive.

Gentle Guidance

Ten principles for respectful behaviour support

1. Behaviour is communication.

2. All children develop at different rates.

3. There is no perfection, only progression.

4. It's to be expected that some days feel harder than others.

5. Looking after yourself is a priority and benefits the children in your care.

6. Feelings are indicators of where we are; it's OK to feel as we do.

7. Behaviour progress isn't linear; it swings back and forth.

8. Celebrate every small win and don't beat yourself up when things don't go to plan.

9. You can implement positive change today by starting small.

10. Gentle guidance will become a way of being over time.

Behaviour-Support Tools and Resources

In this chapter are the complementary tools and resources that will enhance your behaviour support. Included is some further detail on the key concepts and strategies explored throughout the book, along with some extra information on their effectiveness. As ever, these tools and resources overlap, and by practising them consistently, they'll become part of your routine.

You can pick and choose the gentle strategies to try, depending on your child and their needs, but also depending on you, your needs and your current situation. Remember that if you think any strategy isn't working, you will gently remind yourself, with no blame or shame, that behaviour support is a mindset first, and revisit your wellbeing over and over again until it becomes second nature and an integral part of your daily living.

Support tools

I'm often asked by concerned parents, teachers or others who hold supportive roles in a child's life where to begin or how to increase their focus as they support a child. Here are four key areas I always highlight as ways we can increase emotional safety:

- having meaningful connection time,
- supporting a child in overwhelming moments,
- using language mindfully, and
- incorporating small changes into everyday life.

Connection

Taking opportunities every single day to connect with the children in our care helps them to feel important and valued. As we saw in Chapter 4, the ideal minimum is ten minutes' emotional connection time per day when you are fully present with your child, regardless of their age. Do note that any form of emotional connection time must never be used as leverage or punishment, and it should take place daily even if the child has displayed undesirable behaviours. Here are some additional emotional connection strategies.

Connect with words and pictures

Leave a Post-it note in their packed lunch or on their desk with a funny picture or a few words of encouragement or an acknowledgement of achievement. This keeps the emotional connection 'active' in your absence and supports children with transition outside of their home environment.

If you have an older child who has a phone, send them a text message telling them something positive about themselves (find something to highlight even if it's small – remember you're not seeking perfection, but progression): 'You should be proud of yourself', 'You're demonstrating that you're responsible' or 'I love you no matter what'. This provides children with direct emotional connection and helps to balance what it is they hear from you about themselves. Even though you may still need to speak to your child about areas of development, positive connection ensures that their emotional scale maintains its equilibrium.

Connect emotionally when in close proximity

This is a handy one for teachers looking to establish or strengthen connection with a pupil. As they're getting on with work in the classroom, place a supportive hand on their shoulder (provided they're comfortable with that). Explain that you're going to turn a sand timer over on the desk and you'll return to check in on how they're doing (not for work completion, but for wellbeing) once it finishes. And give them a smile (even if they don't smile back!).

For parents, when you're pottering around at home, if your children (of any age) have been in a separate room to you, go and give them a kiss, if they're comfortable with that, as you're passing by, or ask 'Are you OK?' or 'Do you need anything?' This helps children internalise that feeling of consistent emotional connection, as they understand that you are always holding them in mind even when you are not directly with them.

Stop and listen

At least once a day when your child is talking to you, try to stop and actively listen, putting all of your attention onto them. Do not interrupt and instead try to see/understand what it is that they are communicating from their perspective. Provide eye contact with the child (though be mindful that not all children feel comfortable with or can naturally return eye contact, so don't demand it) and try to be on the same level as them, so if they're sitting down, you sit down too. You know the children in your care and their needs best. Children need emotionally available adults, and practising giving them your undivided attention at least once a day helps to balance their emotional scale.

Being there for a child in the moment

The most effective behaviour support is always preventative, and pre-paving the way is the most meaningful and sustainable long-term approach. However, no matter how much progress you are making on the bigger picture of behaviour support, there will be smaller everyday challenges that crop up and test our patience. Here's a reminder of some ways to respond to a child who is feeling overwhelmed and is losing their cool, and how to support them in that moment.

Seen, heard and safe

Imagine a car rolling down a steep hill with the handbrake off. If you were the passenger in the car, you wouldn't choose that moment to ask the driver, 'Why did you put the handbrake down? You should really have thought about that – what could you do differently next time?' As the momentum picks up, in that moment the priority is getting the car under control and getting to the bottom of the hill safely! As with behaviour support, once the momentum has picked up, the priority in that moment is emotional stability and at times, even physical safety.

Validate feelings

Validating emotions is sometimes the most effective way of connecting with a child during a tantrum. Simply listening and repeating back to them what they've said shows them you are there for them, ready to support them. By giving them an outlet for their frustrations or anger, you are immediately offering them the release they need to process their feelings (they're entitled to) and move forward. Offering validation doesn't in any way mean you necessarily agree with them or that it'll change the outcome (so you still won't let them have that ice cream you've previously said 'no' to), it just communicates to them that you see their perspective, which in turn offers them reassurance.

Boundaries and expectations

Knowing what to expect in the form of a pre-agreed boundary and expectation helps a child feel grounded during a moment of overwhelm. Once feelings are validated, remind the child of the boundary and expectation, for example, 'I can see that you are really frustrated about… however, you will get your phone/tablet back tomorrow, as we talked about before.'

It's important during a tantrum that your expectations remain consistent. It's extremely unlikely that in the heat of a moment the child will do or say something to make you feel better – for example, offer an apology or halt the behaviour immediately – as it's difficult to think beyond how we feel. By repeating the expectation and reaffirming the pre-agreed boundary, you are helping to keep the focus on what you're trying to achieve. This can help slow the momentum of a tantrum and stops us from diverting our attention away onto the secondary behaviours that leave us feeling drained and unsuccessful in our behaviour support.

Remain calm

Be what you want to see mirrored back. When a child has reached the point of meltdown, they are unconsciously asking for help to manage their big feelings. They need your steady presence, reassuring voice and unflappable body language. Keep in mind that by losing their cool, they're not trying to manipulate you or deliberately wind you up, and just like you, they're also not enjoying what's happening. Though these episodes can feel never-ending when you're in the middle of them, remember they will end, and the young person will eventually decompress. Maintaining your self-care (page 116) is one of the best ways you can retain your equanimity in these situations.

Supporting through mindful language

The words we say are extremely important and make energetic imprints in our life that stay with us long after the event. This is because words are sounds that carry an energetic vibration and hold power through their frequency. It's why, if you said to a baby, 'I am acutely discontented right now because I'm sleep deprived,' they'd have no idea what the words mean but would feel the vibration of them and understand that Mummy or Daddy is tired and not feeling great! A wonderful compliment or a negative remark made can stay with us, and recalling it can bring about an emotional reaction similar to how we felt in that moment, even if it was a long time ago. On the flipside, if you have said something in the past to someone that you regret, remember no blame, no shame. Blaming and shaming yourself will only have a negative impact on your perspective and your thought, feeling and action pattern. The best thing that you can do for yourself and others is try to understand why it occurred (which is overwhelmingly likely to have been as a result of you not feeling good at the time). We can always change course and act differently, which also happens to be great modelling for our children – it's OK to make mistakes; once again, there's no perfection and only progression.

Given the words we choose have such an impact on our experiences and perspectives, practise being more mindful of language and, more importantly, be aware of the intention behind your words. Ever had someone say they're really happy for you, but nothing in their actions matches those words? As we've looked at previously, children are experts in detecting this! They learn more from what we do than what we say and are often more energetically plugged in than we are, meaning that they are often more attuned to how an environment feels. So, take your time when beginning to become consciously more aware of this, as it can be quite a revelation when we realise the things we say subconsciously on a daily basis and, as ever, maintain your mindset/wellbeing, then watch how positively language can impact on behaviour.

Thank you, not please

When asking children to do or not do something, we often say, 'Carly, please stop doing that,' or, 'Carly can you turn your iPad off now, please?' When we say 'please' it is a request and the young person's brain then subconsciously asks, *Hmm… should I or shouldn't I do it?* When we say 'thank you' the brain receives it more as an expectation that it will be done. So, 'Carly, stop doing that, thank you,' or, 'Carly, turn your iPad off now, thank you.' This is a fun strategy, as it's quick, easy and impactful – there will likely be times as you practise when you say, 'Carly, turn your iPad off now, please – oh, I mean thank you!' Laugh, take on no shame or blame and continue to practise until it becomes second nature.

Language of choice

Earlier in the book, we looked at why offering choice is so important. Regularly providing children of all ages with appropriate choices gives them opportunities to practise self-control over their lives in a supported way. One of the key reasons for undesirable behaviour is trying to get a feeling of control, which makes young people feel safe. This strategy should feel easy to integrate into your life if you start with everyday things such as, 'Would you like to wear the white T-shirt or the purple T-shirt?' 'Are you going to eat the cherry yogurt or the banana yogurt?' or 'Are you going to do half an hour of homework now, or fifteen minutes now and fifteen minutes in an hour?' Ensure that either option the child chooses is agreeable to you. When using the language of choice, two choices are recommended and both options should support children to grow and develop. You wouldn't provide options such as, 'Are you going to play on your Xbox now and do your homework later, or do your homework now and play on your Xbox later?' This is because if they choose the first option, it's unlikely that they will do their homework at all later. A way to decide on your options is considering *How would I feel if they chose that option?* If it fills you with dread or panic, then don't provide it!

The whys behind every request

So often we ask, as if on autopilot, children to do or not do something, and when they respond with 'Why?' we may reply along the lines of 'because I said so', or 'don't answer me back'. In order to pre-pave the way as much as you can, ask yourself, *Why have I requested this of my child?* You may be surprised to realise that much of the time it's because your parents would have issued the same instructions and you've just subconsciously taken on that language. Another reason might be because it simply suits you better in that moment. When I first qualified as a teacher, I regularly asked for complete silence in my classroom. Looking back, I can see that it made me feel in control when everyone was quiet. It felt orderly and calm, as I had a subconscious per-ception that associated noise with chaos. I quickly realised that, for me, control was driven by a fear of feeling out of control. Once I addressed this, my classes changed dramatically and the children under my supervision felt empowered, and thrived, as did I. So consider why we ask what we do of children – and it's OK to change your mind! Even if you've been doing some-thing one way for a long period of time, you have the freedom to change it from today if you'd like to.

Focus on what you want, not what you don't want

Encourage children to focus on the behaviour that you would like to see by consistently highlighting that, rather than what you want them to stop doing. So instead of 'Stop running,' try, 'Can you walk? Thank you.' Instead of 'Stop shouting at me,' try, 'Can you tell me that in a calmer voice?' (Ensure that you model the calmer voice as you speak.) You will most likely have to repeat it a number of times, but notice the incremental pro-gress as the behaviour shifts from undesirable to desirable more quickly over time. If you state what you don't want them to do (for example 'stop running'), it can lead to repeat behaviours, which can dominate in the brain, causing children to begin to associate themselves with the behaviour, believing that's who they are, such as, *I am the child who shouts all the time* or *I am the child who always gets in trouble*. As with all these strategies, take your time and practise them with no blame or shame.

Proximity praise

This involves giving another child, who is displaying desirable behaviours, some attention. This strategy should be used sparingly and its implementation should be soft and subtle. It is really important that emotional connection time (page 214) is a consistent part of your routine before using this strategy, as it should encourage young people towards more desirable behaviour rather than making them feel that they have come up short in some way. So if the emotional connection time is going well and your intention is to gently encourage your child, while you're feeling emotionally balanced yourself, then you may say to another young person in close proximity, 'Thank you for stopping talking when I asked. That shows me you're ready to leave the classroom.' Or, 'Thank you for not interrupting me when I was on the phone. That was very patient of you.' Then the instant you see your child revert to more desirable behaviour, praise them in the same way, even if it's fleetingly initially!

Now and next

Adults' and children's brains are wired differently, and each of us has further distinctions in our brain composition, depending on chemical balance, past experiences and trauma, among others. When I worked as a classroom teacher, I could tell you at any point in the academic year how many weeks and days it was until the next school holiday, which was the longest half term and the shortest, and by how many weeks! I loved my job, but as a parent and teacher I had segmented the year in my mind as a coping mechanism to manage my life. Young people often see their days as one very long road ahead and some children adopt coping mechanisms to move through their day. For those who are very young or for older children who are often overwhelmed by their emotions (manifesting as undesirable behaviours), everyday life can be mind-boggling and the need for control tends to creep in to try and keep the anxiety and overwhelm down. You may have noticed this in surprising situations; for example, if a playdate with your child's friend, which you think will be a happy activity for them, doesn't go well. From your perspective, a chance for them to play with their friend should be exciting and fun, but from theirs, not knowing how to get from where they are now to being able to play with their friend – not in the literal, but the emotional sense – can feel intense and overwhelming. You may be able to relate if you've ever felt apprehensive in the daytime in anticipation of an evening event – once you're there, you might feel fine, but the build-up to it can feel unnerving.

One way to help create a sense of calm and order for young people is to partition the day, depending on their needs, into segments of 'now and next'. For example, '*Now* we're going to have our breakfast and *next* we will put our clothes on.' Or, '*Now* we're going to stop at the shops to buy a dessert, then *next* we will go to Simeon's house.' Partitioning the day into now and next can help children to get through the day emotionally. This language strategy can be supported with a 'now and next' visual, such as a small whiteboard, or even with a visual timetable showing the entire day broken up into segments.

Invite feedback

Language is a two-way street. Being mindful of our language and how we use it helps us to gently guide and support children. Going a step further by inviting their feedback can give us a lot of insight, helping to inform us how to further support them. Should you try this strategy, you must be prepared to really listen to the children in your care.

There's a difference between active listening and listening to respond. When we actively listen, we try to receive what the person is saying to us without judgement or opinion. Active listening is a valuable skill that tends to require practice, so try it with another adult first – you may be surprised to find that it's harder than initially anticipated! Because we are so subconsciously rooted in our perceptions, which are derived from our beliefs, more often than not we listen in order to respond – when someone is talking, we're thinking of what we want to say back to them, what opinion or point we want to get across, rather than just accepting what they're saying as *their* truth. There's no right or wrong here, no blame or shame, just different perspectives. In order for this strategy to be effective – to really hear what your child is telling you – you'll need to receive their perspective without agenda. Then at a later point respectfully consider what's been said and if you are going to act upon any of it. Putting this into practice, you might say to a child of any age, 'Is there anything that you'd like me to change or do differently?' or, 'What things do I do/can I do to make you feel happy?' or, 'Do you feel that you are listened to?'

Afterwards, make no promises but thank them for answering your questions and tell them that you value their opinions so will think about what it is that they've said. It's crucial that you don't undermine their contributions following a question; for example, if they respond saying they don't feel listened to, and you react by saying, 'But I do listen to you!' or, 'That's not fair to say that!' Instead, gently thank them for being honest and reiterate to them how important it is that they feel heard. If a question such as 'Can you tell me why you feel that way?' or, 'What would make you feel listened to?' elicits no answer, don't push them, and rest assured that the guidance in this book in and of itself will support them to feel more emotionally secure over time.

Everyday life

Ideally, behaviour support strategies become embedded into everyday home or school life over time, so we're no longer reaching for a strategy to stop or fix a behaviour. Instead, the strategies are our way of being. They'll eventually feel less like a chore and instead an empowering way to make the behaviour journey more enjoyable. Here are some strategies to work into each day that will provide the kind of subtle, ongoing support that children thrive on.

Social stories

If your child is repeatedly struggling with something such as leaving the park (revisit Chapter 7 for this example), sports day at school or bedtime, pre-plan and practise scenarios with them. For younger children this may be in the form of a story, or role-playing the scenario over and over with them. Use the language of choice and ensure that your expectations and boundaries are clear and consistent – this will support you to gently guide them while giving them safe choice, helping them to be part of the decision. For older children this can be done in the form of a conversation when they are in a good-feeling place and you can gently discuss any effects (or consequences) should they not adhere to what has been pre-planned. The key to success with this strategy is acknowledging and celebrating the incremental progress.

Routines

Routines provide emotional certainty for young people, as knowing what is coming and expected next is very emotion-ally reassuring. Routines can be supported through the use of visual aids that children can manipulate – such as a laminated daily and/or weekly timetable, a calendar or a 'now and next' board, which can have the child's name on it and be hung in their bedroom if they'd like – which in turn promotes inde-pendence and accountability. Ultimately you are guiding the routine, but getting children involved in their creation will give them a sense of ownership. Depending on age and need, you could also create smaller, pocket-sized routine visual aids that you can easily carry around and refer to throughout the day.

It's OK to change or adapt routines (life happens), but try to maintain consistency as far as possible to support young people to internalise the feeling of emotional certainty that routines bring. If changes occur, use the language of choice to emotionally support the child through the change and help them to rebalance via safe control. Be particularly mindful of transitions within routines. Consider how a child will be supported from one part of the routine to the next. For example, if the morning routine at school is to line up in the playground with their classmates and then enter the classroom and get reading books out, some children will need to be supported in the transit from one thing or one space to the next. They may benefit from a numbered space in the line, for example. It may seem like a small thing, but having a particular place in the line rather than having to find somewhere to fit in can be a huge relief from a child's perspective, reducing anxiety and soothing stress that would otherwise manifest into undesirable behaviours.

At home, something as simple as having a warm drink and a set amount of TV time before bed can support the transition from living room to bedroom. Consistency really is the key here. Children will most likely try to change and mould the pre-agreed routine regularly to test the boundaries and check how emotionally safe it is – or you are. Once they realise that it will not change, they will relax into the routines. As ever, be sure to acknowledge and celebrate the incremental progress along the way.

Responsibilities and opportunities

Provide young people with responsibilities and opportunities, and not because 'they need to learn' but because it *feels* good! Often the reason the young people push back against the responsibilities we give them is because they feel 'done to' instead of 'part of', or unseen and unheard instead of valued and respected. No blame or shame – we are all doing the best we can from where we are, and often the responsibilities that we give children are ones that we may have been given as children or that were passed down to us as what is important to help us grow into respectful adults. Nothing wrong with that at all. However, talking to children about why we perceive something to be important that they may not is gentle guidance. Instead of 'You need to do your homework to get a good job,' hook a child in from their worldly perspective and talk to them about what they may want to be/do in life and refer to their current interests. From there, identify how talking about that makes them feel, then link that in to how doing their homework helps them to focus, build on existing knowledge or learn something new, teaches them about time management and helps them adopt new skills. Use the language of choice (page 220) to support them to feel better about that task and to provide them with safe control. Reframing tasks (that could be viewed as drudgery) as responsibilities and opportunities will foster more enthusiasm and cooperation.

Incremental coaching

It can feel frustrating to find ourselves repeating instructions to children over and over again – but remember that by maintaining your wellbeing, frustration will reduce, leaving space to perceive these moments as opportunities to teach and learn. Remind yourself, *It's to be expected that a child, right through to adulthood, will not do things as we would like all the time. It's to be expected that they will test the boundaries. It's to be expected that they haven't learned that yet!* Their brains are developing, and part of that development is repetition and consistency. Isn't it good to know this? It is universal and you are not alone. Be as you would like the children in your care to be. Keep in mind:

- When you're frustrated, how do you communicate to them?
- When you're learning something, how would you expect someone else to speak and behave towards you?
- When you're trying to break or maintain an old/new habit, how many times does progress swing back and forth?
- Model the behaviours that you would like to see from children.
- Tell them that it's OK to slip back, and provide examples of when you've done the same.
- Be aware of your interactions and conversations with others about your child. What is the main focus?
- If you were observing yourself, what gentle advice would you give yourself?

Take it step by step from where you both are rather than where you'd like them to be. Consider what you would like to achieve and then work out the steps that will take you there. Just as you would when a baby takes their first steps, when your child puts one foot forward, acknowledge and celebrate. Then when they fall, help them up to do it again and again until they take another step, and then another.

Alternative ways to express emotions

We are all communicating through our behaviour all of the time. Emotions are energy in motion and, as we've seen, if they don't have an outlet, they can build up and manifest as undesirable behaviours. To support children who are telling us how they feel via undesirable behaviours, we need to provide them with other ways to express their emotions. Consider something expressive that they enjoy – any type of physical activity that gets the body moving is excellent, and music is another good outlet. Art and craft activities or writing are also great to incorporate into daily life.

Breathe

The benefits of conscious breathing are unbelievably positive, as it activates the body's relaxation response. Simply pausing and taking a conscious breath can alter your perspective almost immediately, and becomes more effective as you practise this strategy. Breathe in for a count of five and out for five, through the nose, then repeat this three times. Here are some typical times in the day you're likely to find conscious breathing really helpful:

- in the morning, before getting out of bed;
- before you collect your child from school or they return home;
- as you return from work and begin the evening routine at home (I always take these grounding breaths before starting the evening care for my mum);
- before you react or respond to a behaviour;
- in the car, if your children are arguing in the back seat. Pull over safely, get out and pause, then take these conscious breaths before speaking to them.

Try to do it as much as you can to reap the benefits, but I would strongly advise you do it at least every morning after waking. If you're not convinced, try it – you've nothing to lose!

You'll particularly notice the upside of it when you've been practising for a while, but on one occasion you don't do it (because progress swings) – in a situation like this, observe how different you feel and how this then impacts on how you interact or respond. Once you've practised consistently, you can support young people to do the same.

Resources

Here is supplementary advice on some of the key behaviour-support strategies I cover within the book, along with resources to help you put them into practice.

Emotional stepping stones (page 169)

The stepping-stones resource helps to acknowledge the numerous progress steps that we take but often don't recognise (perhaps because we've been conditioned to see progress looking a certain way). It will take a bit of time to revise your perception of progress if you haven't considered this before, but I promise you, once you do, it's a life-changer for pretty much any and every type of progress in your life.

The first thing you need to consider when working with these stepping stones is that emotions are neither good nor bad. It's the common behaviours often associated with these emotions (such as feeling anger and then acting aggressively) that sometimes lead people to mislabel emotions. The reality is that emotions are indicators either of where we are or of a need that requires addressing. It is OK to feel any feeling – remind yourself of this via repetition, literally telling yourself and the children in your care that 'It's OK to feel as you do.'

As I explained in Chapter 7, it's difficult to release old behaviour patterns. Our brains are designed to take shortcuts and go back to what they know best, even if that presents as undesirable behaviours. These are primal survival programmes etched into our brains that bring reassurance that we are safe – something familiar can feel comfortable, even if that means a low mood. What trips us up is when we blame and shame ourselves or others when we slip back into old patterns, and rather than remembering that progress swings back and forth, we think that our efforts aren't working. Acknowledging and celebrating the incremental progress during these times will help you to keep moving, and although leaps of progress can be made, one step at a time builds a stronger foundation to build upon and steadily progress.

The stepping stones illustrate how we move up from the lowest emotions through to the highest (see the illustration on page 169). Remember, a child needs to feel better in order to behave differently (as do we all). Moving from one stepping stone to another is significant progress along the journey and if each step can be acknowledged as just that, then it'll feel that something positive is happening beneath the surface.

The key with this resource is ensuring that you do not stay on the lower steps for long; being consciously aware of emotions in this way should provide you with the boost to keep moving forward. What you'll find in time is that circumstances in life can take us back a few steps to anger, for example, but if you've been maintaining your wellbeing, that swing back will be brief and you'll swing forward once again through the steps.

Temperature check (page 123)

The temperature check helps children to understand what's happening for them internally that comes out as behaviours externally. It's very empowering for young people and gives them a sense of understanding and control over what often feels like behaviours manifesting beyond their control. The idea is to support children to understand that their behaviour doesn't stem from nowhere or because there is something wrong with them. Their emotions are valid and important and will never cease to exist; however, their behaviour can change over time. The temperature check also helps them understand that there are levels of emotions: there's not simply OK and not OK, or happy and sad, or calm and angry, which is the way young people often describe their feelings to me. If they can identify a whole range of feelings and when they may arise, they can learn in time not to be afraid of them, and not to bury them or project them onto others. Feelings are good! They warn us of danger, tell us if there's something unhealed or an unmet need to be addressed. Equally, feelings can uplift us and others, contributing to a fulfilling life.

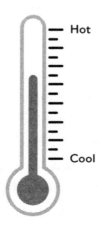

Thought–feeling–action (page 53)

In Chapter 2, we looked at how our perceptions link directly to our thought–feeling–action cycles, so here's a resource to help you or a young person identify them (I recommend that you practise this for yourself first). It will help you see what your subconscious programmes are, by which I mean those patterns of behaviours we find ourselves repeating over and over without really recognising why, or where they come from. When we are more consciously aware of why we do things, we are then better placed to tweak or change our thought–feeling–action cycles, should we choose to.

When you feel ready, start practising this, and begin to think about where your thoughts have originated from. This following case study is an example of a thought–feeling–action cycle at work.

Case study

At the airport I once witnessed a mother shouting loudly at her two children as they zipped in and out of the crowds while waiting to board their flight. Lots of other travellers were shaking their heads and looking on disapprovingly and I could see the mother becoming increasingly on edge and then shouting at the children even more. I purposely sat next to her (as most others had moved away!) and we began talking. She initially told me that she didn't usually shout at her children in this way, but this **action** came as a result of her children acting up and embarrassing her in public. She continued that if her children behaved better, she wouldn't have to shout. As we continued to talk, though, I realised there was more to it. It turned out she hated flying and what's more, she'd never flown on her own with the children before. These **thoughts** had led to **feelings** of anxiety and fear that had kept her awake all the previous night and she was exhausted. As a result of feeling tired, anxious and fearful, her response to the children (the **action**) was to shout at them. This was all perfectly understandable and there should be no blame or shame attached. Simply by being aware of how our thoughts and feelings impact our actions, we are in the position to make a different choice in our responses.

It may sound fairly simple, but it can take a bit of time to utilise this resource effectively, as it means digging a bit deeper to find the root cause of the cycle, especially given 93 per cent of our actions are subconscious! So as ever, take your time and practise: you may be surprised to find where the causes originate from.

Thought	Feeling	Action

Incremental progress

This key resource is one that I always recommend as a priority (along with the next resource, wellbeing watch). The acknowledgement and celebration of incremental progress can immediately transform how we view a situation, by changing our perception and then our thought–feeling–action. Something you may have previously perceived as hopeless can suddenly be viewed in a different light, with progress being made. It's particularly effective combined with the stepping-stones resource (page 169).

Use this resource regularly and consistently, either weekly, fortnightly or monthly and in direct correlation with the wellbeing resource (page 244). Here are some useful ways your increments may be acknowledged.

Time/duration: *A child who used to scream for two hours after being dropped off at school now screams for one hour.*

Frequency: *A child who was walking out of one lesson every day is now walking out of three lessons a week.*

Task: *A child who never remembered to hoover or put the dishes away is now hoovering but forgets to put the dishes away.*

It's paramount that when celebrating increments of progress there is no 'but', for example something like: 'She's improved in that she's no longer screaming for two hours, *but* she is still screaming.' This is because the 'but' can override the acknowledgement of progress and dampen the celebration, causing the continued progress to slow down. The 'but' thought has a knock-on effect on the way you and the child feel, which can then impact negatively on what they do next, and this is why wellbeing maintenance is vital, as it becomes a protection and prevention from returning to negative cycles of thought or behaviour.

	Evidence of incremental progress				Maintaining wellbeing check
Focus behaviour	Week 1	Week 2	Week 3	Week 4	Y/N

Focus behaviour	Evidence of incremental progress		Maintaining wellbeing check
	Fortnight 1	Fortnight 2	Y/N

	Evidence of incremental progress		Maintaining wellbeing check
Focus behaviour	Fortnight 3	Fortnight 4	Y/N

	Evidence of incremental progress	Maintaining wellbeing check	Evidence of incremental progress	Maintaining wellbeing check
Focus behaviour	Month 1	Y/N	Month 2	Y/N

Focus behaviour	Evidence of incremental progress	Maintaining wellbeing check	Evidence of incremental progress	Maintaining wellbeing check
	Month 3	Y/N	Month 4	Y/N

How full are you? (page 119)

In Chapter 4, we looked at how being emotionally full reduces our capacity to offer children effective support. How can we look after others if we are depleted? Taking care of ourselves is the antidote to becoming overloaded, and here's a resource to help you monitor how full you are.

Prior to implementing consistent self-care (see next resource), draw a line on the glass to indicate how emotionally full you think you are now. Then record how full you think you are over time. When a setback occurs that fills you up, record it and continue with your wellbeing practices. The aim is to generally operate at a lower percentage the majority of the time, so that if something significant does crop up and your percentage rises, you are not spilling over.

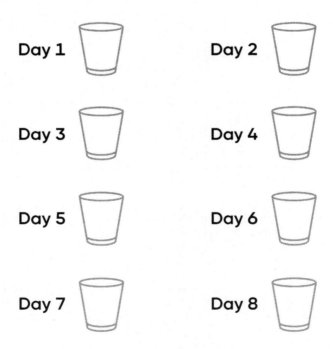

Day 1

Day 2

Day 3

Day 4

Day 5

Day 6

Day 7

Day 8

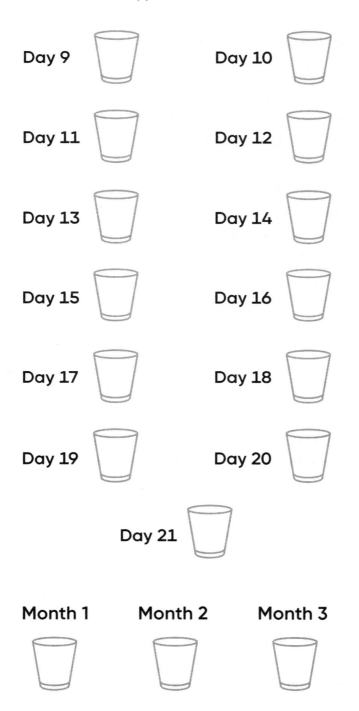

Day 9

Day 10

Day 11

Day 12

Day 13

Day 14

Day 15

Day 16

Day 17

Day 18

Day 19

Day 20

Day 21

Month 1   Month 2   Month 3

Wellbeing watch (page 115)

The beauty of maintaining our wellbeing is that it undoubtedly benefits our entire life and everyone in it. When we're feeling good, we can look at the same person, situation or scenario but perceive it ever so slightly differently (or even drastically so). Similarly, children are much more receptive to adults who are calm and grounded than to a parent, teacher or similar who is losing their cool (no blame or shame).

Start prioritising yourself today, even if it's doing something small, and use this upcoming chart to track and monitor your progress. Consistency is vital, so that it eventually becomes part of your everyday routine, as ingrained as brushing your teeth. Your wellbeing underpins your mindset, which is the most important aspect of behaviour support.

Choose anything that makes you feel good and maintain the consistency. Here are some ideas should you need them:

- Have a warm drink every morning, when you can mindfully enjoy each sip in solitude (even if it's just for five minutes).
- Take a long or brisk walk around the block (whatever you prefer or can manage on a given day).
- Reserve bath day(s) for yourself and if you can, indulge in your favourite bath products.
- Make time with pets: if you're an animal lover, stroking pets can be very soothing.
- Read a book (actual books rather than something on a screen) – this can feel like a real me-time treat.
- Go for a drive, if that is something that you enjoy.

- Listen to old favourites or discover new music or podcasts.
- Phone a friend or meet up with that person you've been trying to catch up with for ages.
- Stock up on your favourite food or drinks.
- Get those endorphins going by doing some exercise. If you've never been a fan of exercise, find a type of movement you enjoy (it's out there, I promise).
- Do something for someone else.
- Give someone a compliment.

Wellbeing practice	How do you feel?		
	Day One	Week One	Month One

Emotional connection

This resource is a way of ensuring that emotional connection time is planned for and consistent. On page 214, I suggest devoting ten minutes per day to uninterrupted connection time but, depending on your current situation, a quality two minutes at least three times a day may work better for you. It may not sound like a lot, but two minutes of you remaining totally focused on the present moment may feel long at the start! Don't give up on it, though: it can be really effective and bring glimmers of light into the relationship between you and a child.

Ensure that the young person in question feels like they have joint ownership over this time. It should be relaxed and enjoyable (it may take time to ease into this if you haven't been doing it this way). Only do what feels comfortable for you both. Here are some suggestions:

- listening to music together
- dancing
- playing
- talking
- telling jokes
- looking at photos
- baking
- driving
- shopping
- walking
- going for a bike ride
- working on a jigsaw or a video game

Emotional connection time	Yes	No
Sunday		
Monday		
Tuesday		
Wednesday		
Thursday		
Friday		
Saturday		

You can also access a printable version of all the resources found in this chapter at www.bloomsbury.com/gentleguidanceresources to use at your leisure.

Epilogue

You might have come across the well-documented concept of the growth mindset and the fixed mindset. Coined by renowned psychologist Dr Carol Dweck, this theory says that people fall into two categories. If you have a fixed mindset, you're likely to see your skills as something innate, rather than believing in the power of hard work or practice. In turn, you might avoid trying new things for fear of failure, or give up easily when something doesn't initially go to plan. All of these thoughts then form core beliefs, which can impact upon how you then perceive things. When life doesn't go your way, you are self-critical, seeing yourself as a failure. Rather than enjoying the successes of friends or colleagues, you might immediately compare your life to theirs.

On the other hand, a person with a growth mindset tends to give new challenges a try and if they don't immediately succeed, they don't admonish themselves but instead try again, seeing setbacks as a learning opportunity. They believe that with a bit of effort, even if what they're aiming for doesn't come naturally, they'll get there. They're inspired by other people doing well, rather than feeling threatened by their achievements. They fall off the horse, dust themselves off, then get back up again.

I'm sure you can see where I'm going with this. Dr Dweck's research into growth and fixed mindsets is applicable for every age and stage of life, and coupled with an understanding of our beliefs and why we perceive as we do, I believe it is the cornerstone of behaviour support. The great news is that even if you've veered towards a fixed mindset in the past, you can change that. Can you imagine how the flexibility of a growth mindset could give you the confidence to try new methods of support, even if you've done things in a different way before? Do you see how it would help you to embrace new challenges, viewing each one as a learning opportunity? How it'll give you the resilience to bounce back from obstacles and, rather than dwelling on mistakes, see the opportunity to take another approach next time?

Being in the right mindset is everything when it comes to behaviour support, which is why it's the main focus of this book. We're all doing the best we can from where we are. That includes you – you are enough and you are doing enough. Simply by reading this book your behaviour support progress has begun.

From here onwards, I'd like you to remember you have the power of choice in any moment nurturing a child; a bit like one of those choose-your-own-adventure books, the options of how you gently support your children lie with you. This responsibility may feel a little daunting at first, but it's ultimately empowering. If you've been supporting young people in a particular way for years, you have the power of choice to change or adapt, should you choose to. If you've been perceiving things in certain ways all your life, you have the power of choice to alter your perceptions, should you choose to. If negative thought–feeling–action cycles have been dominating your experiences more than you even realised, you have the power to create new cycles and so do the children in your care. Remember that a shift in mindset can shed a whole new light on how you can respectfully guide young people.

You can only offer so much guidance with words: action is the real teacher. When you gently integrate the practices within this book into your life and begin to embody them, the children in your care will witness first-hand the behaviour you'd like for them. They will learn to prioritise their own wellbeing when they see you prioritising yours; they will learn not to apportion blame or shame when they see you living by the mantra; they will learn not to be afraid of emotions but instead become curious about them. Above all, they will learn to become who they are meant to be, their inimitable self, with strong foundations for a life of joy and purpose. They will learn that they can unlock their own fulfilment, relying on themselves rather than others or material possessions.

I'd love this to become a book you return to, hopefully getting something new out of it each time you delve in. Be mindful that we have just as much to learn from young people as they do from us – their inspiration lies in their not wanting to become like us; they want to carve out a new path, and so they should.

Be the change you want to see – you've got this!

Further Resources

Books

I have found these books and their authors hugely inspirational.

John Bowlby, *A Secure Base: Parent-Child Attachment and Healthy Human Development* (1988)

Louise Michelle Bombèr, *Inside I'm Hurting: Practical Strategies for Supporting Children with Attachment Difficulties in Schools* (2007)

Shefali Tsabary, *The Conscious Parent: Transforming Ourselves, Empowering Our Children* (2015)

Philippa Perry, *The Book You Wish Your Parents Had Read (and Your Children Will Be Glad You Did)* (2019)

Dr Carol S. Dweck, *Mindset: Changing the Way You Think to Fulfil Your Potential* (2017)

Organisations that provide additional support

If your child has additional needs, these national UK-based organisations are good places to start when you're looking for sources of support.

Action For Children, www.actionforchildren.org.uk
National Autistic Society, www.autism.org.uk
Scope, www.scope.org.uk

Sense, www.sense.org.uk

The Key Clinic, www.thekeyclinic.co.uk

UK government website help pages, for example, www.gov.uk/help-for-disabled-child

You can also access a printable version of all the resources found in Chapter 10 at www.bloomsbury.com/gentleguidanceresources to use at your leisure.

To follow Marie Gentles, or for further guidance, please visit www.gentlesguidance.com or find her on Instagram, @mariegentlesguidance.

Acknowledgements

I am so grateful to the people and experiences that have shaped me into who I am, and provided me with the knowledge and wisdom to write this book.

Firstly, to every single young person that I have had the absolute pleasure of working with, I truly mean this from the heart: I have learnt as much from you, as you have from me. Your feelings are valid and your voices are heard, and I will continue to model resilience, positivity and love, no matter what.

I would like to sincerely thank my previous colleagues with whom I've worked alongside since the beginning of my teaching career, but especially to my amazing staff when I was a headteacher. We happily went above and beyond to support the young people in our care, as exhausting as it was at times, and there are no regrets whatsoever. Strategies to gently guide young people were implemented and developed from some of the most high-level behaviours in dysregulated young people, which literally changed them and their families' lives for the better.

Thank you, Luigi, for reaching out and having faith in me. It was destiny when I realised that you were the first agent for my favourite author!

Thank you, Bloomsbury. What an amazingly supportive team! I feel so blessed.

Finally, to my mum who will never know how much her and my dad's love and guidance has given me the confidence to finally be bold enough to speak my truth. From a quiet, shy, young girl to a woman on a mission to unite, empower and support others with no blame or shame.

Dillon and Tamera, I love you.

Index

A Note on the Author

Marie Gentles OBE is one of the UK's leading child behavioural experts. A former head teacher at a pupil referral unit, she is a behaviour adviser to the Department for Education, an educational consultant and parent. Founder of Gentles Guidance Ltd, she trains schools and family services in her bespoke method to set up positive foundations and practical ways to support children through disruptive times. She was a behavioural expert on BBC's *Don't Exclude Me* series. *Gentle Guidance* is her first book.